Also by Serina Bird

*The Joyful Frugalista: Grow Your Cash, Be Savvy
with Your Money and Live Abundantly*

THE JOYFUL STARTUP GUIDE

THE **JOYFUL** STARTUP GUIDE

Now is the time to make your
startup dreams come true

SERINA BIRD

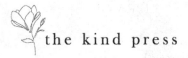

the kind press

Cover design: Christa Moffitt, Christabella Designs
Editing: Georgia Jordan
Internal design: Nicola Matthews, Nikki Jane Design

Cataloguing-in-Publication
entry is available from the
National Library Australia.

NATIONAL
LIBRARY
OF AUSTRALIA

ISBN: 978-0-6452626-7-4 paperback
ISBN: 978-0-6452626-8-1 ebook

To my husband, Neil, who edits all my podcasts and grounds me when I'm carried away with big ideas that I have no idea how to implement.

And to anyone who has ever dared to bring a dream to reality.

Foreword by Avril Henry

What an absolute delight this book by Serina Bird is! Like Serina herself, the book is full of tips, good advice, wisdom and humour shared in a simple and uncomplicated way, with a great dose of generosity.

What I love about Serina, and it shines through this book in bucketloads, is that she is optimistic and a realist, she is passionate and a dreamer, she is visionary while always being practical and realistic, she is a change agent, yet never overcome by failures or challenges—she picks herself up and tries again and again until she succeeds. She has the heart of a lioness, a strong work ethic, compassion, and a deep commitment to helping others in life and in succeeding.

If you are ready to pursue your dream of being an entrepreneur, self-employed and living your best life, then this is the book for you. This book is like unlocking a treasure box of checklists, tips, tools and advice from someone who has been there and succeeded (and failed), and always believed in the possibility of her dreams and ideas—at times terrified, but always stronger in her self-belief than her fear!

The book is practical and flows from one logical process to the next. It is the perfect step-by-step manual on how to start up your own business.

I wished something like this had existed when I started my own business in 2003; it would have made starting a business as a single mum, who gave up a highly paid corporate job, much easier and far less stressful.

In this book, Serina effortlessly moves through the different stages of a startup business, with sound advice about what to do, what to watch out for, and even what to avoid. My favourite parts of each chapter are the thoughtful and insightful questions and practical exercises to stimulate your own thinking about what you truly want for your business, your values, objectives, goals, aspirations and outputs. Follow this advice and answer each of these questions truthfully, and you cannot possibly go wrong.

This book is an invitation to follow your dreams of being an entrepreneur, your own boss, owning your own business, doing work you love that feeds your soul, nourishes your heart, expands your thinking and creates the blueprint for living your best life, not anyone else's! Accept the invitation, and as Serina advises, don't wait until things are perfect. Enjoy the journey!

Avril Henry
Founder
Avril Henry & Associates

Foreword by Diane Phillips

Hello, my name is Diane Phillips. I'm a senior lecturer in Entrepreneurship and Innovation at the University of Canberra, Australia. My own journey has involved startups and exit strategies, and I now see myself as an innovator and intrapreneur in the university I work for.

I met Serina through our local Canberra Innovation Network events, such as the Canberra Female Founders series. Inspired by Serina and her network, the Female Founders events are all about passion and purpose, and participants' discussion is purpose-driven toward social impact through innovation and entrepreneurship, plus the power of collaborating and networking with women-led businesses throughout the Australian Capital Territory and beyond.

Having gotten to know Serina, it's hardly surprising that her second book, *The Joyful Startup Guide*, has come to fruition to support up-and-coming entrepreneurs.

Serina's passion and enthusiasm come through in everything she does. You will see this in the book as Serina, a storyteller, shares her knowledge, skills and wisdom as she continues to grow in her own innovative and entrepreneurial journey, learning and growing through every aspect of business life. The ten chapters of the book cover the preliminary steps 'Before You Jump Ship', to the basics of getting started in your business—such as planning and branding, building trust and networking, joining the startup/business ecosystem, basics of finance, productivity, co-production and teamwork—and the final chapter, 'Ready, Set, Launch!'

Providing the reader with a broad overview, what to do and tips from her experience to smooth the way for future entrepreneurs, Serina herself and the book explore and demonstrate the energy, enthusiasm and hard work needed to get a startup to market.

Another important aspect of the book is that Serina is honest and transparent as she demonstrates her ability to learn, fail and fall, and shows the steps to bounce back up with resilience and as a stronger business person. With grace and substance, Serina shows her growth in leadership, knowledge, and great determination to succeed. All-important attributes for start-up ventures.

Serina has a focus on women in business, reminding me of some of my own experiences mentoring women who want to be in business and have a strong desire to be independent. The main element for me has been to support them in terms of confidence in their own vision and business understanding, whilst managing a family and job and planning their future dreams, in a common-sense way that the book does.

The Joyful Startup Guide provides strategies, responses and actions to alleviate the challenges/obstacles/roadblocks that women face when starting up their entrepreneurial ventures as women in business. In addition, Serina's book looks to reduce the invisibility of women as entrepreneurs, sharing success stories and providing role models for future female entrepreneurs.

Serina's Joyful brand, her books, podcasts and courses not only enable others to dream big and follow their dreams, but also inspire Serina herself to continue on her journey as a writer, podcaster and innovator.

Diane Phillips
Senior Lecturer, University of Canberra
Program Director for the suite of Bachelor of Business Degrees
Chair of the Canberra Business School Seminar Series

CONTENTS

INTRODUCTION

**Warning: this book may make you quit your job.
Or do something radical.**

I don't mean to encourage people, especially women, to quit their jobs in the search of living a life aligned with their true purpose, but I tend to have that effect on people. And I'm not sorry.

This is not a book about how to grow a six-figure business in a week. I do have a fabulous entrepreneur friend who successfully started a new business with a $100,000 contract. And others who are doing even better.

But I'm still in the start-up phase, still finding my groove, and not *yet* attracting rivers of gold for my ideas. I am, however, manifesting it to come. I have big dreams, and already I'm seeing the proof that it is happening.

This book shares some of my newbie learnings to help others as they flow and grow into doing what they feel soul-called to do.

MY STORY

Just over two years ago from writing this, I quit my diplomatic career. I didn't take leave without pay, and I didn't take long service leave—I just *quit*.

It is almost unheard of for people to do that. In China, they often refer to public service careers as the iron rice bowl (*tie fan wan* 鐵飯碗): it's an income that is unbreakable. The reality is that changes, mergers and redundancies do occur—but for a mum with two young kids to support, it's a stable and secure choice.

My decision to leave work was to a large extent forced by my being in a difficult and toxic work section. It can happen anywhere. I'm not about to criticise my former department, and in fact, I later went back to work there (I talk more about this in Chapter 7). I am, arguably, more sensitive to conflict and stress than many others due to some lingering PTSD from my first marriage. Leaving work when I did provided me an amazing opportunity to heal and grow and to lean into doing what I love.

Simply put, it was time.

ON *FIRE*

My decision to leave work was influenced by the Financial Independence, Retire Early (FIRE) movement. When I started writing about saving and investing in my book *The Joyful Frugalista*, I wasn't consciously part of FIRE. I had even said publicly that I *wasn't* FIRE. I enjoyed my job, was good at it (even though I didn't think so at the time) and dreamt of having a dual writing/public service career while being fabulously wealthy.

The FIRE movement coopted me. I began to read about and meet with some amazing people in the FIRE community. What I love about the movement is that financial security and independence shows how people can live life on their terms and do what they want. YOLO—*you only live once.* People on FIRE say no to conventionality and do what they want to do.

A week after the toxicity at work hit a pinnacle, and while I was still beating myself up about not being thick-skinned enough, I went to Sydney and participated in a panel discussion after the screening of *Playing with FIRE* hosted by share-trading platform Pearler. As I watched the first-person story of a couple who decided to quit their jobs and pursue financial independence, a little voice inside of me whispered: *Why don't you do that too? What use is money in the bank if you can't use it to make your dreams come true?*

By this stage in my life, I had remarried my super-supportive husband, Neil. Neil had spent over thirty years working in the public service, and had strong work security and great super. I also had good super, the home mortgage was almost paid off, we had investment properties, we owned our car outright and had no personal debt. I didn't quite fit the profile of most people who hit FIRE, but I was close enough that I could take a risk.

In a way, it might have been easier and perhaps more conventional if I had decided to retire rather than go into business land. In the early days, it might even have been cheaper, and certainly safer. But I'd always been that person who dreamed of being in business. I love innovation and always found myself scribbling random business ideas into the back of diaries or notebooks—anything I could write on really. I was an out-of-the-box thinker. But, in my public service land, the thinking was (of necessity) so risk-averse it was like working in a secret box within a locked box.

MY BUSINESS MODEL GOES BUNG!

Before I left, I had a simple (and I thought effective) business model: become famous and earn lots of money.

It's easy to laugh at that, but there was some truth to this. I was getting a fair bit of media following the publication of *The Joyful Frugalista*, had four freelance writing arrangements and had launched a podcast with a friend that was tracking well. I planned to work with that friend to develop other ideas, one of which (eventually) formed the genesis for *The Joyful Business Club*. (I discuss partnership pitfalls in Chapter 8.)

For the first few weeks, things did well. I picked up a new freelance writing arrangement, worked on promoting the podcast and spoke at various events.

Then things changed.

The first was the bushfires, which started three weeks after I quit. With Canberra blanketed in toxic smoke haze for months, I was mostly trapped indoors with my kids. It wasn't the best environment for writing mojo, although it did motivate me to start writing about giving away items in a challenge I termed Joyful Giving.

Then the podcasting partnership busted up at the end of my first post-work month. I hadn't predicted it, but with the benefit of hindsight, I knew I should have. At the time, I was devastated, as a large part of my post-work business model was going to be fleshing out some of my ideas with someone I thought was a close friend and business partner. Now it was all kaput.

But setback is an opportunity for growth, and after encouragement from friends (special shoutout here to my big-sister friend Trish Smith and the lovely Erna Glassford, aka @simplycheecky), I had the courage to launch a solo podcast in early March, with my husband, Neil, as producer. In mid-March, COVID started to bite and podcasts trended. Two weeks after launch, *The Joyful Frugalista* podcast was featured in *The Canberra Times*. It's since been profiled in *New Idea* as one of three top finance podcasts, and has also been highlighted in *Money Magazine*. I love, love, love being a podcast host and I learn so much from sharing the wisdom of my amazing guests.

Then, during COVID, many of my freelance writing gigs started to dry up. My writing resonated for lean times, but unfortunately (like many creatives) there just wasn't the money to pay me. A lot of advertisement revenue dried up and that affected the bottom line for what agencies could pay contributors. If I wanted to write for free, there were a lot of opportunities.

I did think about taking a volunteer approach as I was close enough to financial independence for it to be a hobby. I spoke to friend and business advisor Janine Linklater. 'Should I just do it as a hobby?' I pondered. She convinced me to continue working towards building a viable and sustainable business (these days, businesses). And yes, it is possible.

As paid writing opportunities dried up, I did two things. One was to start thinking about what kind of support I could offer entrepreneurial women. The second was to start running training courses, including my signature Six Weeks to Abundance with The Joyful Frugalista course.

For the former, I reached out to a friend I knew to explore a partnership. That went for a few months before it went bang—spectacularly. Let's just say I now have a lot of wisdom to share about what could go wrong with partnerships, which I explore in Chapter 8.

It was, once again, horrid, and in the aftermath I wallowed in self-doubt. But again, I used the setback as an opportunity to move forward. Part of the dissonance was that I felt we weren't on the same page, so I started to think more about my vision and values. Within days (and with thanks to Neil for his suggestion), I rebranded as *The Joyful Business Club*, built a website and launched a Facebook group, where I now host weekly Facebook Lives. The content and experience of these Facebook Lives, including the incredible people I have interviewed, form the bedrock of this book.

And regarding courses, I have discovered I love being a course facilitator almost as much as I love podcasting. Whenever I get off a course coaching session, I am buzzing. I light up, and I love seeing how I have that effect on others in the group. It is such an amazing privilege to help women and men reach their potential. I feel like this is what I am called to do.

Another setback was saying no to my 'Savvy Shopper' column that ran for several months in 2020. And I had several other associated gigs, including recipes and editorials for *Australia's Best Recipes*. 'Savvy Shopper' was a high profile, full-page spread, and it also led to six appearances on *Studio 10* and some great radio interviews. I'd be crazy to say no to that, right?

Yes, I'm crazy. It's hard to explain exactly other than I was feeling angry and anxious about it. It wasn't my brand and it wasn't on my terms. It felt like being back at work again, except for less pay. I didn't feel my values were aligned; I was upset one day to read (what I considered to be) a racist opinion piece in the same paper as my article. Once again, there was a misalignment of values.

While saying no to big, blingy publicity might sound crazy to many, I felt that I had become disconnected from my tribe. I felt I was so busy being 'out there' that I wasn't listening and connecting. I still don't listen enough, but hopefully I am becoming more authentic. And writing this book, based on the feedback I am receiving from my tribe, is one of the steps in that process.

Could I have had more setbacks? Yep, I could. In 2021, I set out to develop a second-hand clothing marketplace called *The Joyful Fashionista*. A friend recommended a website developer, who ended up being dodgy. The work he performed was so bad the website didn't even rank in Google and had to be pulled offline due to major security flaws. It was a costly exercise in terms of money, reputation and community confidence—and also in terms of expending negative energy to get out of the relationship and rebuild.

But I didn't let it deter me. I went back to my values and core principles. Through that, I reaffirmed that I was deeply passionate about sustainability and loved fashion. The deeper belief behind it is that, with the right clothes, every woman is truly beautiful. I decided to develop the website myself and relaunched *The Joyful Fashionista* in December 2021. And the gift in this is that I'm now passionate about educating myself and others about tech to help prevent these types of problems.

WHAT THIS BOOK IS ABOUT

This book is not an expert guide on how to be mega-successful by someone who has made it and can reflect on a long career. I'm a business newbie, and I'm still learning and growing. Rather, this book aims to capture real insights about what I have learnt and wished I had known before leaving my career, and the steps to get started. I want to save you from making the mistakes I made.

This book aims to tell it as it is.

In the same way that people (especially women) rarely have honest discussions about money, people rarely talk about the realities of doing business.

Most businesses fail.

Yet most business owners are proud to have had the courage to follow their calling.

During COVID, I interviewed my friend Marg Wade, author of Canberra Secrets and founder of Canberra Secrets Personalised Tours, on whether she had any regrets about leaving her public service career. Like many people in tourism, her business has been crippled. 'I have no regrets,' she said.

Carpe diem—seize the day.

Wishing you wealth and happiness in following your heart-centred business journey.

Serina

Connect with me on *The Joyful Business Club* Facebook page and group.

HOW TO USE THIS BOOK

This book is yours to use how you wish. It's been structured around ten chapters, which mirrors the ten-week Mastermind classes I run through *The Joyful Business Club*. The ten weeks represent a school term, with the idea being that it's a good-sized chunk of learning without being overwhelming.

Throughout the text, you will see a series of positive affirmations in boxes. These are designed to provide you with an affirmation you can use to help you navigate and overcome any blocks in your entrepreneurial journey. If something resonates with you, write it down and repeat it to yourself often. I like to write down affirmations on Post-it notes and place them on my computer so that I can encourage myself during difficult times.

You will also find frugal tips and other tips. These are super handy little things I've learnt and discovered that will help you save time and money. It's surprising how many little things can trip you up when you are starting out!

And at the end of each chapter, you will see a series of exercises. I suggest you buy yourself a special notebook, one that is beautiful and sparkly or speaks to you with its sustainability or message. Write out the questions—and answers. Come back and review what you have written from time to time and observe the magic of your journey as it unfolds.

1
BEFORE YOU
JUMP SHIP

If you are reading this book, I'm guessing it's because you have a business, idea, charity, social enterprise or startup you want to work on. Maybe you've been thinking about it for a while, or maybe the flash of inspiration has just taken you. But whatever it is, you are probably keen to get started.

I know. I hear you. I'm an impatient 'let's get going and do it NOW' sort of person.

But before you go all-in, this chapter sets out the importance of following your passion, and some practical things to consider before jumping ship.

BUILD YOUR SIDE HUSTLE

Sometimes you might decide to do a burn-the-boat exit from your work. Maybe you feel you need to because the work environment is toxic or not aligned with your values. (That's pretty much what happened to me; I had planned to leave in a few years, but in the end, the decision was made and executed within twelve months.) Or maybe you took a gap in your career due to caring responsibilities, or travelled, or moved overseas to accompany a partner.

But the wisest thing to do is to follow my mum's advice and always have a trump card up your sleeve.

Growing up, we played a lot of cards. I especially loved 500. And a key rule of that game is to hold on to your trump cards, because you never know when you might need to pull one out at a crucial moment.

The same goes for life. It's generally best to wait until you have a new job lined up before you quit your current one. And it's generally a good idea to start building up your business on the side before you branch out on your own.

Even if you do have financial savings (and I recommend you do), suddenly going from a regular salary to nothing can feel daunting. And even if you have savings and investments, your salary can be a security blanket holding you back.

I've suffered from putting myself under too much pressure to suddenly create an abundant, profitable business within a short timeframe. Some people manage to do this, but the vast majority don't. It's much better to ease into business by starting something on the side first. If you have a supportive workplace, you can even look at reducing your work hours to gradually focus more on your business.

Building a side hustle before you jump ship also gives you time to test some of your assumptions about your business, build a customer base, and develop business systems. Having something more organised than a shoebox for your receipts can keep your accountant happier at tax time—and also give you a clear snapshot of how your business is performing.

The big problem, though, with building your side hustle (especially for women) is that you risk burnout. Many women are already superwomen juggling many responsibilities—and that's before there is a side hustle on top of that. Sometimes women can overwork themselves because they misinterpret professional as meaning working 'hard'. And yes, I'm guilty of this. I've taken my laptop on cruise ships and even camping. I've written much of this book during a COVID lockdown while homeschooling and with hubby away for work.

WHAT'S STOPPING YOU?

This isn't a rhetorical 'just do it' or 'dream big' question so much as a practical one. Are there any things in your work conditions or contract that stop you from building your side hustle or future business plans? For instance, if you are planning to set up a business that will compete with your boss, it is important to check your employment contract carefully to see if it has a non-compete or restraint clause. It may even be worth getting legal advice about what you can and cannot do. You risk being sued and shut down if you are in breach of your contract.

It's also worth considering whether your side hustle might create a conflict of interest with your current job. It's probably not appropriate for a police officer, for instance, to moonlight as a bouncer at the local nightclub. It might seem okay at first. But what if there was an assault—or worse—and the police (your colleagues) were called?

I worked as a public servant for twenty years. I had to sign an annual conflict-of-interest form. I also had to declare any outside employment, including side hustles, blog writing, freelance writing, and volunteer positions in service organisations such as Zonta. This might sound like overkill. But imagine if I wrote a blog post criticising an aspect of public policy, and a news agency liked it and then paid me to run it on their channels. 'Serina Bird, public servant, says the Government should not have done [XYZ] ...'

It's not a good look. My boss would not be impressed. But more seriously, I would likely be reprimanded, or worse, lose my job. And fair enough, as my opinions would have been formed from my daytime work, including confidential information that I had access to (even if I hadn't quoted it).

Don't let this happen to you. Think clearly about what your business or startup is going to be about and how you might navigate any potential conflicts of interest before they arise.

LOOK FOR WORK AND TRAINING THAT WILL PREPARE YOU FOR YOUR BUSINESS

If you know you are planning to leave your job at some point and set up shop, think about the type of roles and training that you can do now to help you develop the necessary skill sets. I'm not suggesting you breach conflict of interest or steal clients. Or do anything disreputable. Rather, use it as an opportunity to consider skill sets you can acquire now that will enable you to shine in your current role—and also prepare you for the future.

For instance, much of my business relies on social media. While I've done my own social media training (e.g. attended ProBlogger twice), I also attended a fabulous course many years ago about how to use social media in a public policy context. I've utilised many of the skills from the courses I have taken myself, as well as work-sponsored courses and materials, to make a positive contribution when using social media in a work context. I've often gone above and beyond in the social media space because I like and enjoy it. But also, there are lessons from my work experience (and the course I did) that have informed my business. Win-win.

Writing and leadership courses, in general, will give you skill sets that will help in your current work role—and your future business. And if you want to get into coaching or training, you could put yourself forward for training roles, even if they are not in your usual area or background. You might end up with training certifications or liaising with training organisations. The knowledge of how to develop and deliver training could be useful, even if the type of training or work you do is in a completely different specialisation. For instance, you could volunteer to provide orientation courses or ICT training, and then later become a life coach or lead spiritual healing workshops.

In *The Beginner's Guide to Wealth*, Noel Whittaker shares how taking up a work-sponsored opportunity to improve public speaking eventually led to a successful career as a bestselling author, finance commentator and writer. At the time, few employees took up the offer, with most choosing instead to enjoy more free time. Noel's work now influences around three million people a week.

OBSERVE AND RESEARCH

Start using your time to research trends, look at your competition, and above all, listen and observe. What are people around you talking about? What are their concerns? What is the media talking about? You might not yet be able to say, 'I'm about to start a business doing [XYZ],' but you can start tuning in to the frequency of what is happening around you.

In my case, I began to tune into what people were saying about money. Young people were concerned about saving for a deposit to buy houses; upset about 'smashed avocado brunch' rhetoric. People I worked with started to dabble in ETFs. And there were many discussions about frugal food and the rising cost of energy bills. Sometimes, these topics (in a modified form) made their way into my book or other writing.

HOW DO YOU IDENTIFY YOUR PURPOSE?

Perhaps a key blockage for you is you're not sure about your life purpose. A bit like waiting for Mr Right, maybe you are looking for the 'right' business before you get started.

Maybe you expect your purpose to fall on you like a big neon sign. 'Serina, THIS IS YOUR LIFE PURPOSE …'

Some people do receive a calling. For some, it may be the voice of God telling them to choose a vocation. But for many of us, the answer may seem a bit opaque, but also, in retrospect, obvious. Simply put, you probably already know the types of things that are aligned with your values and purposes, but recognising the answer is an exercise in self-awareness.

YOU ARE NOT DEFINED BY WHAT OTHERS WANT YOU TO BE

There is so much societal pressure to choose a career that defines you. Do you remember being in primary school and people asking you what you wanted to do when you grew up? In Asian cultures, it can sometimes start even earlier. For instance, when my sons turned one and we were living in Taiwan, part of the celebration included encouraging them to crawl towards objects that would indicate their future career (e.g. calculator equals accountant, microphone equals singer). And of course, parents would try to encourage their baby to pick up the things that would indicate a professional career that could earn lots of money.

I recognise I'm writing from a position of privilege, as a university-educated woman from a middle-class background in Australia, one of the most prosperous countries in the world. Not everyone has the luxury of being able to quit their job and lean into their passion project; I didn't have the courage when I was a single parent going through divorce.

> *I can live the dream I imagined as a child.*

But I do want to say that career and business opportunities are changing so rapidly that the concept of sticking to a career for life is no longer true for many people.

Just think—ten years ago I asked my sister whether or not it would be a good idea to sign up for Facebook, yet now there are many jobs for social media managers. There are many opportunities for people to build lucrative social media and marketing consultancies, promote their products on social media, or even earn money as influencers.

WE EACH HAVE UNIQUE GIFTS

Every one of us is different and has unique gifts. For instance, I like talking (I used to be nicknamed the mouth of the south when I was young). I also like learning foreign languages, writing, doing Facebook Lives, and coaching. I also like organising events and thinking about entrepreneurial ideas. I get so excited by possibilities!

My husband, Neil, likes technical things. During the global pandemic, he built computers for each of my sons (and two of their friends). He likes tinkering with electronics and loves watching videos about trends in cars.

Neil despairs of my inability to plug things in properly and my struggle to make it to events on time. But when it comes to talking to people, negotiating, sorting stuff out or setting the vision, he leaves it to me.

WHAT ARE YOU GOOD AT?

You know it, but you likely don't know it. And that's because sometimes we have been programmed to keep those socially unacceptable gifts a secret. We are often educated to be compliant and do the right thing.

For instance, because I had good marks at school, it was expected that I would go to university and study law. This wasn't due to pressure from my parents. I was raised in a liberal environment surrounded by creatives who have not been to university (my mother was a successful fashion designer and businesswoman who left school at age fourteen). But it never crossed my mind as a teenager that I might one day leave a defined career to do things like write books, develop recipes and launch a startup.

During my first marriage, I started to have radical ideas about wanting to leave the public service and do entrepreneurial and/or media things. But I wasn't able to act on them. Since my divorce, I've been reconnecting with who I am as a person and what I enjoy. I remember now how I excelled at speech and drama at school (even though I didn't think I'd ever been a good actress because I didn't look like a supermodel), how I loved creative writing, how I always had lots of ideas, and how I tended to take a leadership role in groups. At home, I loved to cook and was always experimenting.

Now, when I write, record podcasts, speak at events or conduct coaching, I light up. I start to glow with the passion of what I'm doing. I can see it sometimes in myself when I look back at video footage I am in.

I light up with joy when I do what I love.

FOLLOWING YOUR HEART-CENTRED MAGIC

A good way to find out about your gifts and exploit innovative ideas is to get in touch with your intuition.

Yep, your intuition. A hunch. Your divine guidance. Your spirit guides. God. The Universe. Whatever you call it, I'm talking about that nudge you get sometimes. That sudden idea that floats into your mind when you least expect it, that refuses to go away and leaves you feeling oddly excited, wanting to research how to make it happen into the middle of the night. (In my case, it often pops up when I am working on an urgent deadline.) *Maybe I could ... What if ...*

Have you had one of these moments? For some people, it leads them to start developing a new business—often successfully. For most of us, it's just one of those things we push aside only to find, years later, that someone has taken the same idea and built a profitable business from it.

For years, I had a list of 'maybe' ideas scribbled in the back of my work diary. Yes, I was always professional in my work and went above and beyond. But while others were zoning out during industry sector briefings, my mind was lighting up like a Christmas tree, thinking, *Oooh, next big trend, I wonder if ...*

In his book *Think and Grow Rich*, Napoleon Hill talks at length about the power of our mind in attracting prosperity. According to Hill, our brain is both a broadcasting and a receiving station for the vibration of thought. 'MAN'S ONLY LIMITATION, within reason, LIES IN HIS DEVELOPMENT AND USE OF HIS IMAGINATION,' he says.[1]

Hill goes on to talk more about what he terms the sixth sense. To him, it was something that defied description, yet was important (vital even) in attracting abundance. 'There comes to your aid, and to do your bidding, with the development of the sixth sense, a "guardian angel" who will open to you at all times the door to the Temple of Wisdom.'

For me, the 'sixth sense' comes in many different forms. Often, I will just *know*. Usually, I feel a sense of joy. Sometimes, I feel tingling in my body, especially my hands. Sometimes I feel a deep, warm sense of wellbeing in my stomach. Often, I will feel positive, elated and excited.

While you can't force your sixth sense to produce ideas, there are things you can to do promote this, like listening to and validating the signals it sends you—even if they are small ones like 'phone a friend—now'. Meditating, walking, swimming—all these things can put you in the zone where you can receive messages. When you look after your body and are not driven by anxiety, you allow your brain to pick up on other messages.

DID YOU KNOW?
Shower power

Up to seventy-two per cent of us get great ideas while in the shower.[2] It has a lot to do with the joy we get from having a shower. When we are relaxed and happy, and our brain is releasing dopamine, we are more likely to come up with good ideas.[3]

I like to think there is something meditative and zen about the sound of flowing water, and spiritually, the symbolism of washing away the clutter and dirt and letting in the new. But whatever the reason, it works. Next time you are in the shower, allow your mind to wander and see what ideas you come up with.

Bec Cuzzillo, business coach and founder of the Spiritual Business Academy, talks often about the need to listen to this intuition. Genuine, spiritual intuition is different from that inner voice of doubt that often follows. She advises her clients to concentrate on their energy when these different voices run in their heads. What is positive energy that makes you light up? What, instead, brings you down?

Bec has a clear message for all aspiring heart-centred entrepreneurs. 'Your magic is so needed in the world,' she says. 'You've started a business because you felt called to serve, to make a difference in the world, and show up for those you want to support in a beautiful way. You need to answer that calling and to step up and share your magic.'

> *I am a heart-centred leader.*
> *My magic supports and uplifts others.*

YES! AND …

Before you take an idea and say, 'Nah, it would never work,' just stop. Right there. Now, let's reframe the conversation.

Around five years ago, I attended a training course at work run by Google. (Another example of how work-related training has helped me later in life.) As part of it, we were encouraged to solve a problem with out-of-the-box ideas. We had many different coloured blocks of Post-it notes and different pens. We had a deliberately short window of time. As we slapped down ideas, we were instructed not to comment negatively on ANY idea.

Have you ever been in a work meeting when someone came up with a sudden, seemingly whacky and random idea? How did people respond? Most likely, the boss/facilitator/old guards all said, 'No, but that wouldn't work because of [XYZ],' or 'In my experience, that wouldn't work because …'

What happens then is that the person who came up with the idea is discouraged, due to groupthink, from contributing new ideas. They might become silent and withdraw from participating. They may get fed up and leave the project—or even the organisation.

Maybe the person was a bit crazy, but to paraphrase Billy Joel, it just may be a lunatic you're looking for. Crazy ideas have a way of opening up new ways of thinking.

I am open to new ideas and ways of thinking.

To avoid stymying new ideas, in this exercise, we were expressly forbidden to say no to anything. Instead, we all said, 'Yes, and …' when commenting on other ideas. That then created a synergistic effect where even the introverts in the group, who had been holding back, began contributing new ideas. (I often find that the quiet ones, who observe intently, have unique insights that can be easily overlooked.) The conversation then changed to, 'Yes, and we could even go one step further and ...'

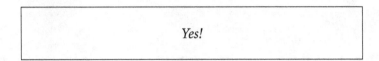

Yes!

Just think of the technology we are now surrounded by. My late nana grew up without things we take for granted, like a television and a bathroom inside the home. She never understood what the internet was, she didn't have a mobile phone (let alone a smartphone) and she never travelled overseas. Yet her great-grandchildren grew up swiping their tablets and both have now taught themselves basic coding (one is into animation). The rate of technological change is faster than she could have imagined, and who knows what next big leaps are out there. We can no longer afford to say 'No, but' in an era where we need and crave imagination and new ideas.

> Do you say *Yes, and* to yourself when you get a hunch or an idea? Or do you say *No, but*? Or do you share your idea only for your partner or friend to say 'No, but ...' leading you to shelve it?

VALUES

One way of thinking about your purpose and how to align it is to also think about your values.

What is important to you? There is no right or wrong answer, but it could be several things, such as:

- Sustainability
- Community
- Family
- Health
- Equality
- Abundance
- Adventure
- Curiosity
- Beauty
- Helpfulness
- Honesty
- Justice
- Spirituality
- World peace
- Collaboration
- Service
- Curiosity
- Loyalty

When I was unhappy in my career, I started to think about what my values were. I realised that behaviours in the work unit I was in were not aligned with my values. No wonder I wasn't happy! Strangely, when I returned eighteen months later, I discovered—as I was doing my induction training—that many of my core values were part of the organisation's mission statement. Yet, still, I didn't feel they rang true. Sometimes there is a disconnect, where the stated core values of an organisation don't filter down.

Identifying what your core values are will help you identify the type of work—or business—you want to be in. For instance, if you value sustainability, you might not be happy working at a company that makes disposable products and does not commit to finding more sustainable solutions. Starting up your own business and making an environmentally sound alternative might bring you joy instead.

According to Bec Cuzzillo, people who feel the call to be in business are often connected with the call to live aligned with their purpose and values. 'It's about sharing our magic with people in a way that allows us to live a life of meaning and support others to do the same,' she says. 'We can have beautiful, heart-centred businesses where we are living our purpose and are stepping into our higher vision for ourselves and our lives.'

I am living in accordance with my values.

EXERCISES

1.

What things do you currently like and enjoy about
your study or the work you do now?

2.

What would you like to do more of?

3.

What are your values?
Can you identify at least three?

4.

Keep a notebook for a month and write down all
the business ideas and possibilities that come into
your head. Do not dismiss anything as crazy or
ridiculous.

5.

What are the words others use to describe you?
Listen carefully to the positive things people say
about you and what you are good at and write them
down in your notebook.

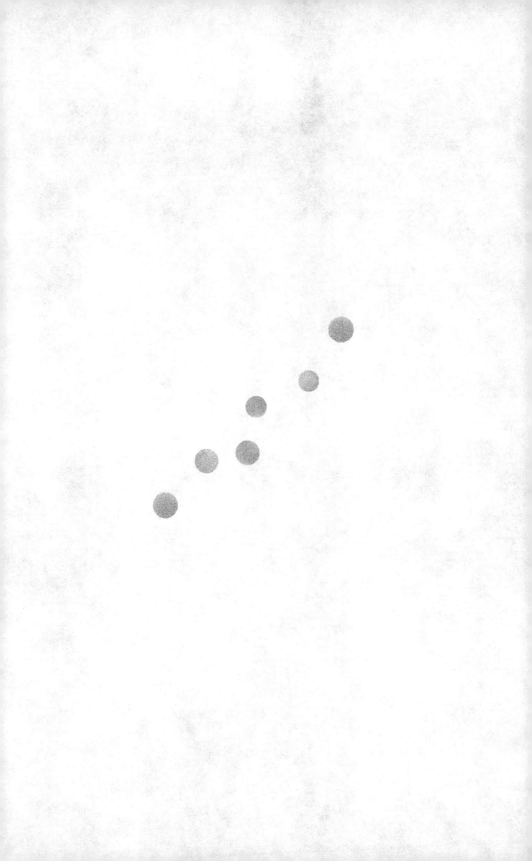

2
BUSINESS
SET-UP BASICS

You've thought about what you are passionate about. You're following your hunch or intuition. You might even have a few ideas for a business name. Now what?

In this chapter, I'll outline some of the practical things you need to do to get registered, be tax compliant and get going in business. You don't have to do everything all at once, but it is important to do some things (such as getting your socials and domain name set up) before you do other things. The key thing here is to take imperfect action and get started.

WHAT'S IN A NAME?

Do you have a name in mind for your business? Or are you still not sure?

The name for your business could be one of the most important decisions you make. The name will say a lot about your 'why', and what you are trying to achieve.

But how do you decide if it's the right one or not? Here are a few of my tips.

1. **Ask your tribe.** You might like the ring of a new name, but what do your potential customers think? Ask your friends, or even better, put out a poll or feelers on social media. A good way to do this is on a Facebook group such as The Joyful Business Club. My experience is that people LOVE commenting on things like names and logos, especially if you give them a choice.

2. **Consider the appropriateness of the name.** Have you ever come across a business that has an acronym that is, well, a bit rude? Or has a potential double meaning? You might not have a dirty mind, but others may. Ask someone you know who is a bit cheeky (in my household, it's my husband). Run the name past them and ask for their honest opinion about whether there might be anything rude, laughable or inappropriate. Also run it through the *Urban Dictionary* to check for slang phrases—especially in other places such as the USA. You would be surprised how many truly unfortunate business names there are (and how many people may snigger but not own up to why).

3. **Search the internet for similar names.** This is especially important when we get to registering social media and domain names, but do it first before you run off and create a logo.

4. **Trust your intuition.** After you've run your potential name past other people, ask yourself: *What feels right for me? Why?* At the end of the day, it's going to be your business and you want to feel proud when you say its name. How does it feel when you say your business name? Does it roll off your tongue? Or does it feel a little bit weird?

It feels good when I say the name of my business.

---

5. **You can always change your business name.** Many big brands have changed their name to fit with a new direction, and within my circle, I know of at least two businesses that have recently changed their name. It is best not to change your business name if you can: there is so much goodwill associated with a strong brand name, and there are costs associated with changing branding (and not just with stationery). But it's not impossible

and it's not the end of the world if you do (I discuss this more in Chapter 4).

DOMAIN NAMES

Have a cool business name? How would that translate into a website domain name?

Before you go further, it's important to buy up the domain name you want. It might also be a good idea to buy up associated domain names or even names you might need in the future.

Think of it like *Monopoly*: it's all about ownership. Once you buy the right to a URL, no-one else can use it (unless they pay you for it). Remember also that it's important to renew your URL when it is due (usually annually), or else you could lose the right to use your website name.

Many sites specialise in selling domain names. At the time of writing, some of the sources were:

- Namecheap (from $8.88 per year on sale)
- GoDaddy (from $10.95 per year)
- Crazy Domains (from $14.69 per year)
- Domain.com (from $9.99 per year for a .com site)

I often like to buy my domain name through the website building platform WordPress. It has a range of pricing, but generally, it costs around $24 per year.

If you plan to build your website, WordPress is a great option. Buying a domain through WordPress as you are building a website will save you a lot of time and effort. To me, it's worth the additional costs if you are a website newbie, as it can be fiddly for a non-expert to go from buying a domain name to using it to develop their website. That said, I've pointed a domain successfully to a server more than once—and it's easy to do when you know how.

.COM, .NET OR .COM.AU?

When I first started blogging, I was told that it was best to always use a .com URL, as that way it was clear that I was creating a universal platform. But that standard advice might not be the best for your business. It largely depends on what your business is, where it is located, what it does and how it wants to appear.

Website developer Jacqui Owen often advises her Australian clients to choose a .com.au domain name. 'Only businesses registered in Australia can apply for a domain using .com.au,' she says. 'This means that if you see a *.com.au* website, you know that the business is legally registered in Australia. And that's a good thing for Australian businesses wanting to show they are legitimate.'

These days, your choice of domain extensions is broader than just .com or .com.au. There is now a dizzying array of choices, which includes everything from .garden and .fishing to .restaurant. My website for *The Joyful Business Club*, for instance, is at joyfulbusiness.club.

Before you choose something unique, it's worth considering how the domain extension is commonly used. For instance, .life is often used for memorial purposes. And .org is usually associated with not-for-profits and community organisations.

GET SOCIAL

A decade ago, building a website was considered the first step in starting a business. But now, many businesses successfully operate just through social media channels. An advantage of doing this is that social media pages are quick and easy to set up and generally have minimal (or no) cost.

Like websites, social media handles get taken quickly. So even if you don't plan to immediately begin populating a Facebook page or posting to Instagram, catch your social media assets early. It is fine to have and to hold them, but if someone else takes them, then it's finders keepers.

Unlike website domain names, it is free to acquire a social media channel. You can include business details on your page, including your opening hours, and you can even sell through Facebook and Instagram. Some businesses do most of their business via Facebook or Instagram.

The disadvantage of relying too much on just social media, though, is that—unlike with a website—you don't own the asset. As many people discovered during a dispute between Facebook and the Australian Government—where Facebook turned off many Facebook pages—you don't really own your page: Facebook does. The same is true of Instagram, Twitter, TikTok and many other social media channels.

AUSTRALIAN BUSINESS NUMBER

If you are carrying on or starting an enterprise in Australia, you can register for an Australian Business Number (ABN). You can't just register an ABN for fun or just in case—you need to be genuine in planning to be in business or already be in business.

It's generally a good idea to register for an ABN as you are planning your business, even if your activities are only small. You will find it a lot harder to deal with your potential suppliers or customers if you don't have one. For one thing, your customers will expect to see your ABN on an invoice. The good thing is that it's not hard to apply for one.

Make sure you have your tax file number and other details, such as your Australian Company Number (ACN) or Australian Registered Body Number. Head for the Australian Business Register (abr.gov.au > For Business, Super funds & Charities > Apply for an ABN) and follow the prompts.

TIP

Can't remember your ABN? Or not sure if you are registered for GST (goods and services tax)? The Australian Business Register has a handy tool called ABN Lookup. Simply type in an ABN, ACN or name and it will quickly search for available businesses. It's also a great way to check the status of a business you are dealing with.

SOLE TRADER

If you are starting with a side hustle, or a small business, generally the easiest thing to do is register as a sole trader.

According to tax and startup specialist at PwC Damien Hollingsworth, most people usually set up as a sole trader when they first put their business hat on. This is because setting up as a sole trader is the easiest and least costly way of getting into business. Damien advises many startups on their corporate structure; but closer to home, his wife (a psychologist) operates as a sole trader. And for the purposes of her business, that suits her fine.

The key advantage of registering as a sole trader is that you don't have to set up a separate entity. You don't need to establish a company, you don't need to worry about corporate obligations, and all you need to do is tick a box when applying for your ABN.

The big disadvantage is that there isn't a separate legal entity. 'You are the business,' says Damien. 'This means that if something goes wrong, you might be liable and all of your assets—including your home, could form part of any payment to creditors etc.'

SHOULD YOU REGISTER FOR GST?

Unless you anticipate that your business will earn more than $75,000 per year, you are not required to register for paying the goods and services tax.

Most sole traders starting out usually opt not to register for paying GST. This is because, if you tick yes to paying GST, it triggers reporting requirements. And who wants more paperwork when they are starting out? If you are registered for GST, you need to complete the Australian Taxation Office's (ATO) business activity statement (BAS) either monthly, quarterly or yearly.

TIP
How to manage GST if you are a sole trader

If you are registered for GST, for every sale you make, you must charge GST on top of the sale. For instance, say you are selling jewellery for $100. You would need to charge GST on top of that, so accordingly, the price to the consumer would be $110.

If you are registered for GST and do not charge the additional ten per cent, you will need to wear some of that cost yourself. For instance, if you forgot to add GST and only charged $100 to your customer, you would need to absorb $9.09 when it came to tax time. To calculate GST in a figure, divide the total by 11.

According to Damien Hollingsworth, while registering for GST creates an additional reporting requirement, for some startups, it can bring benefits—principally, you can claim back GST. In most cases, the net cost to a business that incurs GST is the GST exclusive amount. 'For a lot of startups, it makes sense for them to register for GST even if they are not at the point of selling because those costs will be reduced by the amount of the GST.' Damien explains that if you are paying money for lawyers, getting advice from accountants and so forth, then those costs could be reduced by the GST that you can claim back.

According to business advisor Janine Linklater, businesses such as restaurants that have large levels of initial outgoings for set-up would benefit most from registering for GST early. The benefits would be less beneficial for service businesses such as professional consultancies where the main expenses relate to personal income.

FRUGAL TIP
Sole traders and superannuation

According to Damien Hollingsworth, sole traders have traditionally contributed little or no superannuation. This is because they are investing all their money into the business. 'Their business is their superannuation,' he says. In his experience, founders run their startups on the smell of an oily rag—especially in the startup phase, and there is little extra to put into superannuation.

Yet superannuation is one of the best investment structures, especially from a tax perspective. Damien suggests startup founders consider investigating superannuation carry-forward provisions that came into effect from 2018. These provisions mean that people can make up to a maximum of $27,500 in concessional superannuation contributions each year and carry forward this unused cap for up to five years. This means that if you have not been able to pay much or any superannuation in the past, you can catch up over five years. Many startups who haven't been able to pay themselves superannuation may choose to use this if their company has a liquidation event or earns a solid income.

REGISTERING YOUR BUSINESS NAME

Once you have your ABN, you will need to register your business name. You can register your business name online with the Australian Securities & Investments Commission (ASIC).[4] Before registering, think of a few different names that you might want to use for your business.

Unless you are trading under your own name, it is an offence to carry on business under an unregistered business name. You only need to register your business name once, as the ASIC register is national and applies Australia-wide.

TIP

You can search for a business name on the ASIC website. If you want a particular business name, it's generally a good idea to search for the name before you register it to ensure it is still available.

asic.gov.au > Use our online services > Search ASIC's registers > Companies and organisations > Check name availability

---

It is straightforward to register a business name through the ASIC website, especially if you already know that your business name is available. You can also register a business name through the Australian Government's Business Registration Service, which means you can register your business name just after applying for an ABN. Make sure to renew your business name when it falls due to avoid becoming unregistered.

FRUGALISTA TIP

Several private service providers will register a business name for you, or you could get your accountant or solicitor to do it for you. But it is quick and easy to register online. It costs $37 for one year or $88 for three years to register or renew a business name with ASIC.

Note that private service providers routinely send out notices several months before business name renewals are due. Read the fine print: usually, it is not a letter from ASIC. You can renew your business name more cheaply by heading to the ASIC Connect website (asicconnect.asic.gov. au). By way of comparison, the amount quoted on a letter I received recently was $99, yet the cost via ASIC Connect was only $37.

FRUGALISTA TIP

I recommend buying a domain name, then registering your business name. The reason is that private companies will often buy up the domain names of recently registered businesses. Within a week of registering The Joyful Business Club with ASIC, I was inundated with letters from private companies offering to sell me domain names. Most of these were around $99 (or more), which was much more than it would have cost had I purchased before registering my company.

The exception to this is if you want to own a .com.au domain. You will need to register for an ABN to show that you are a business operating in Australia before registering for this domain name.

SETTING UP A COMPANY

A company is its own separate entity. Even if you gave birth to it, it now has its own identity. This means that, unlike operating as a sole trader, anything that happens in the company stays in the company. Well, mostly. There are a few exceptions to this.

According to Damien Hollingsworth, while a company structure will usually protect you from losing personal assets in the event of a problem, its separate entity structure means that removing funds from the company is not straightforward. 'You can't just take out money even if you are the sole shareholder and director—without potential negative tax consequences,' he cautions.

Damien advises his clients that there are three ways to remove money from their company:

1. **Pay yourself a salary.** This means you need to become an employee of your own company. The company will be required to withhold an amount from your payment for taxation, known in Australia as the Pay As You Go (PAYG) withholding system. This means that, once you have a company, you have tax obligations, including income tax for your employees (even if you are the only employee). The company may also need to pay the superannuation guarantee for employees and will be liable for worker's compensation, a compulsory statutory form of insurance for all employers that provides protection to workers if they suffer a work-related injury or disease. Your reporting requirements will also include issuing a payment summary to your employee/s. And as an employee, you would need to lodge a personal tax return.

    Because treating yourself as an employee creates a raft of obligations, Damien does not usually recommend businesses adopt this tactic—especially if they are in the start-up phase.

2. **Pay yourself a dividend.** If you are a shareholder, you can pay yourself a dividend. Damien advises against paying yourself a dividend until your company is making a profit and has decent

net assets. If you are the sole shareholder, the dividend becomes income and you would potentially need to pay income tax on it when lodging your tax return with the ATO.

3. **Taking a loan from the company.** Damien says taking a loan from your company 'can be a minefield'. He also cautions the ATO can deem that a personal expense the company pays on your behalf will be a loan. Treatment of company loans is technical, but essentially, Damien advises that if you are loaned money by a company of which you are a shareholder, you must set up a repayment obligation. Generally, you must repay over seven years. If you do not set up a repayment schedule, the amount of the loan will be included in your taxable income. For instance, if your company loans you one hundred dollars and you don't repay it or enter into a repayment obligation before the company lodges its return (or is due to lodge its tax return), that one hundred dollars will be included in your personal tax return as an unfranked dividend. 'It can be a pretty nasty tax result, so it is something to be aware of,' warns Damien. 'If you are taking money out of your company as a loan, make sure you repay it by the end of the year or you enter into one of these loan arrangements.'

It's important to note that if you are the director of your company (or any company), you must ensure the company meets all its obligations to pay its employees (including things like PAYG withholding and superannuation). While the company is its own separate entity, for some corporate responsibilities, such as paying employees superannuation, directors can be personally liable.

Further, the ATO has made it easy for employees to report companies for doing the wrong thing—and the penalties that you could face personally are considerable. Employee superannuation is generally due on the twenty-eighth day after every quarter.

PARTNERSHIPS

Partnerships are an arrangement where two or more people decide to be in business together. It is often used in professional arrangements, e.g. legal or accounting partnerships. Partnerships remain one of the main business structures in Australia. It is also one of the most fraught. (I discuss partnerships and collaborations more in Chapter 8).

Partnerships are generally cheaper to set up than companies in terms of structure. It is worth investing in legal expertise to make sure you know what you are getting into. Unlike companies, all partners are liable for the debts of the business. That means, if one of your partners doesn't do the right thing, you could be left footing the bill. You could also lose one or more friendships over a partnership. Accordingly, it's important to assess the personal characteristics of your potential partner or partners carefully.

Some key features of a partnership are:

- It requires an ABN, just like a sole trader or company
- It has minimal reporting requirements
- All partners share control and management
- A partnership tax return must be lodged with the ATO each year[5]

TRADEMARKING YOUR COOL NEW NAME

If your business name is integral to your business and your product, you may wish to trademark it. You can do it yourself using the IP Australia website, or you can get legal advice. It's worth doing your research before you begin to make sure your trademark is in the right category.

At the time of writing, IP Australia has been going through modernisation and upgrading. I've noticed that in the space of months, its website has become easier to use. The website now has more resources that explain the process and help guide users to choose the right category. It costs $250 to register for each classification number. You need to understand what your business is about before you start picking through the list. For instance, is a fashion business about bespoke design, manufacturing clothing, or selling online? These could all mean that the core business falls within a different category.

If your brand is likely to trade internationally, it is worth getting advice on that as well. Certain markets, such as China, have first-to-register laws and that means opportunists can often snaffle up foreign company names and register them—before they even start selling and marketing to China.

You might wonder if getting your business name trademarked is worth it. If you are a home-based hairstylist who is well known in the neighbourhood, it might not be the end of the world if someone decides to use the same business name. Your customers know you and they will still be loyal no matter what your name is.

And in many cases, founders or companies might decide to rebrand because their business model has changed or the name no longer feels right. I know of several founders in my business networking circles who have changed or are about to change their business name. It can be an expensive process to rebrand, but it's not the end of the world.

But consider the impact on your business if a competitor deliberately acquires your business name or logo. It may be worth the relatively small initial investment to safeguard your business.

BUSINESS LICENCES

One of the things people often worry about when starting a business is the requirement to gain licences. Australia has robust safeguards in place to help minimise risks on everything from food poisoning to asbestos. But it can feel overwhelming and scary to navigate it at first. What if you start a business without the proper licences? Would the authorities shut you down?

Thankfully, the Australian Government's *business.gov.au* website has a useful resource that allows you to search for the types of licences and permits you might need for your business.[6] For instance, when I searched cafe or restaurant, I found:

- Australia New Zealand Food Standards Code
- Dining Music Licence
- Children and Young People (Employment) Standards
- Australian Standard AS 4736-2006: Biodegradable Plastics—Biodegradable plastics suitable for composting and other microbial treatment

CASE STUDY
The Ugg boot trademark case

Most of us know what an ugg boot is. And many of us probably own a pair (or two). In winter, the sheepskin boots are a fashion essential for many people living in the cold capital of Canberra where I live. They are, to many people, quintessentially Australian.

Accordingly, Mr Eddie Oygur of Australian Leather in Western Sydney was shocked when he was sued for trademark infringement by US footwear manufacturer Deckers after he sold a dozen ugg boots to the US. Not only that, but a Chicago Court ordered Mr Oygur to pay USD450,000 in damages for selling the twelve boots.

The word Ugg was registered in the 1980s by an Australian entrepreneur, who later sold the trademark to Deckers. Deckers now owns the Ugg trademark in many jurisdictions, including the US and the UK.

DID YOU KNOW?

If you want to know more about taxation and how it might impact your business, you can sign up to the ATO's Small Business Newsroom newsletters. The bulletins contain links to news articles (and even podcasts) relevant to businesses starting out. And it's especially useful to know if they are focusing on a particular issue during a taxation year so you can ensure your records fully address that. For instance, if the ATO issues advice that this year they will be looking at working-from-home expenses carefully, it can give you a prompt to ensure all of your receipts and information related to working from home are up to date before tax time.

EXERCISES

1.

If you don't already have a business name, take yourself for a walk (or other exercise) and focus on possible names. Have fun with it!

2.

What business names might you want now or in the future? Once you have a list, consider buying up those domain names to ensure you have them.

3.

Take a business friend out to coffee
(or have a Zoom chat) and ask them about
how their business is incorporated.
a) How did they go about it?
b) Would they have done anything the same?
Differently?

4.

Sign up to receive regular Small Business Newsroom emails from the ATO.

5.

Join The Joyful Business Club Facebook group.

3
THE BUSINESS PLAN

Benjamin Franklin famously said, 'If you fail to plan, you are planning to fail!'

But Napoleon Hill, the author of prosperity manifesto *Think and Grow Rich*, repeatedly urges people not to wait for a plan before starting on their abundance journey. To confuse further, Hill then includes a whole chapter in the book about the importance of organised planning.

IMPERFECT ACTION

Taking imperfect action is one of the most important mantras for entrepreneurs.

I first heard the term 'imperfect action' from blogger Darren Rowse at his 2015 ProBlogger event. As he addressed the more than seven hundred participants, we all pledged to go forward and take imperfect action in our blogging—and lives.

I took that mantra to heart. I immediately wrote it (imperfectly) with one of my kid's coloured textas and put it on the fridge. Over time, the colours started to run and I replaced it with a new imperfectly written mantra.

Without leaning into imperfect action, I would never have:

- Started a blog
- Written *The Joyful Frugalista*

- Applied to go on a life-changing creative writing course
- Applied for grant funding
- Started *The Joyful Business Club*
- Begun a podcast—and recorded some amazing episodes even with technical problems
- Tried online dating—which led to me meeting and marrying my husband
- Started coaching

As I mentioned in Chapter 1, when your intuition is nudging you, it's important to validate that by acting on it. Now. Without delay. Even if only symbolically. If you don't, you will always have regrets. As Napoleon Hill also says, 'Do not wait. The time will never be "just right".'

I trust my intuition and act immediately when it calls me to action.

Business coach April Mack says something similar. 'It is important to take the least possible time between coming up with an idea and starting to do it,' she says. 'The Universe likes speed. When your intuition, God, the Universe, your spirit guides, or your "hunch" has a message for you, it's important to trust it. And then act on it.'

What happens when you don't act on your intuition straight away is that you begin to second-guess yourself. *Maybe it's not such a great idea,* you start to wonder. *It's going to take a lot of time and effort—and the more I research competitors, the more I see that this has been done before.*

And then other people start to talk you out of it as well. They haven't had the intuitive nudge that you have had. They don't feel the energy, can't see the vision and it's not part of their consciousness. You have to show them by doing.

When I start a new venture, I purposely imagine myself putting my hands over my ears and going 'La la la' at any negative thoughts. I take action and do something a bit scary. Maybe it's starting a Facebook group or a website, or asking someone amazing to be a podcast or Facebook Live guest. It feels thrilling, like going out on stage in front of thousands of people and hearing their applause. But it also feels scary, like opening your mouth to speak in a comedy routine and worrying no one will laugh.

Then I pause. I sit with the fear. I sit with the idea. Then, after a while—maybe even a few days or a week—I do a bit more. I go further into uncharted territory and dare to do something more. This second time, it doesn't feel so scary.

> *I can do this. I AM doing this.*

I usually start this process without a robust business plan, although often I will have ideas. Sometimes these ideas will literally be written on a paper napkin at a cafe. Other times, the ideas might be mind mapped in big letters on a piece of butcher's paper. Or maybe I just sit at my computer and start writing dot points—like I did when planning this book. Often I like to create Excel spreadsheets with to-do lists as the ideas start to come together.

TOO MUCH PLANNING?

Conventional wisdom is that you need to do a business plan *before* you start a business. There are many sound reasons for this. A good business plan can save you the heartache of spending time doing the wrong things to grow your business. It can help you to map strategically what you need to do, when and with whom, and how much money you might need to spend at first.

Some people, especially those who are naturally organised and like planning, need a business plan before they will feel comfortable starting a business. If you are the sort of person who likes strategic documents, doing a business plan is a great way to start.

And some businesses need robust planning. In my case, most of my businesses are in the digital space, so it's all about beginning to grow by doing. But if you were buying an existing business, or building something complicated, you need to plan.

But according to business adviser Janine Linklater, who teaches business planning processes, 'If you do too much planning, the risk is that you spend all of your time planning and none of your time implementing.'

Business and career coach Bec McFarland agrees. 'People get caught up in having to have a plan, and that means they are planning rather than doing,' she says. 'Also, in the early phases, having that extra responsibility holds you back because it's another thing to add to the to-do list. It can be a huge thing to embark on.'

I once had an English teacher at high school who would spend so much time talking about what we planned to cover during that class, that the bell would ring before we had started to discuss the book that we were supposed to analyse that term.

Can you relate?

Sometimes, if you are the sort of person who (like me) gets affected by imposter syndrome, the more you plan, the more you start to freak out. It's hard to answer questions around future revenue and customer avatars when you don't yet know the answer.

> *I am planning the business of my dreams,*
> *and turning those plans into reality.*

START PLANNING—NOW

As cryptic as it sounds, it's important to take imperfect action *while also* starting to plan. Napoleon Hill advises people to 'begin at once to put your imagination to work on the building of a plan, or plans, for the transformation of your DESIRE into money … Carry out the instructions best suited to your needs, reduce your plan to writing, if you have not already done so. The moment you complete this, you will have DEFINITELY given concrete form to the intangible DESIRE.'[7]

Janine Linklater says that despite the risk of over-planning, in her experience, most of her clients haven't done nearly *enough* planning. When they come to her, she usually sees the key problem is that they are working long hours doing things that are not strategically aligned to their core business goals. In other words, they haven't yet thought about what they want to do and are burning out trying to do everything.

Bec McFarland suggests one approach to overcoming this dilemma is to wait until you have been in your business a while and then write a detailed business plan. Having done a business plan training session with her, I understand where she is coming from. At that stage, I had thought more about my business and so was able to engage with my business plan with more confidence and knowledge than if I were just beginning.

WHY HAVE A BUSINESS PLAN?

According to Janine Linklater, there are a number of reasons you might need a business plan—one person might want to have a side hustle or hobby (working full time and selling at the markets on the weekend), whereas someone else might be aiming for a multi-million-dollar startup with hundreds of employees.

If you are seeking funding from a bank or an investor, the plan will need to be quite detailed and you will need to focus on getting the financial details as close to accurate as possible without overstating them; but if the plan is to provide personal direction for the growth of your business, then you will likely have more focus on the strategic and marketing components of your plan.

Whatever the reason, having a well-rounded document that covers all aspects of the business is going to help you in ways you may not be able to envisage now.

Janine says that the advantage of having a business plan is that it helps people understand what they need to do in their business, where their gaps of knowledge or skills are, and the areas they need to work on. A business plan should be a living document that evolves as the business grows—it is not meant to be a 'set and forget' document.

Bec McFarland notes that companies seeking funding, such as from a bank, often need to provide a business plan. Serious investors may also want to see a business plan for a startup or company, and sometimes you might need one when applying for a grant (or at least the elements of your business plan, such as competitors, revenue model, and funding). I find that having a business plan helps when I write grant applications, as I already have written answers to questions around what my business is about and the problem it is solving.

According to Bec, a business plan becomes especially useful if you grow to have more than one employee or partner. The plan ensures that everyone is working off the same page and that you have shared objectives.

A strategic advantage to a business plan is that it ensures the tasks you are working on are aligned with your longer-term vision. It is useful to revisit the plan every quarter or six months to check that what you are doing day to day is going to achieve the vision. Used in this way, the plan serves to motivate and align. 'Anytime you need a reminder of why you are here and what you are doing, the plan will help,' Bec says. 'It can be a good thing to review at those times when you need a bit of a kick in the pants from yourself to help you get back on track.'

PLAN ON A PAGE

One way to start planning is to use a one-page business plan. The Southern Region Business Enterprise Centre (SRBEC) has a course that involves giving people an A3 piece of paper with question boxes. Attendees write directly onto the piece of paper, and two hours later, they have the foundation of a business plan.

I attended a session at the SRBEC a few months after I had left work. It was transformative. Just in those few hours, I had several epiphanies about where I wanted to take my business and what it was about. I emerged feeling like I was, finally, in business.

According to Janine Linklater, the one-page business plan is a good starting point for business owners. 'If you do a Google search about business plans, you get 40, 50, 60-page documents and it is quite daunting. They contain lots of terms that you probably don't understand,' she says. 'The one-page business plan helps you identify the fundamentals. If that's all you ever do, it's better than nothing, however it's really only the start.'

Having done the searching for a business plan exercise myself (before developing my own, which you can find on my website at joyfulbusiness.club), I understand exactly where she is coming from. There is so much angst about getting the 'right' business plan template and doing it properly. It feels like some specialised art form rather than a tool to help and grow your business.

Janine advises that the plan on a page could be a start in the strategic planning journey of most businesses. 'It is critical to develop your plan further and expand on the fundamentals you identified in the one-page plan, but many business owners don't even do that. Realistically they should be revisiting their business plan regularly.'

Janine suggests focusing on the following core strategic elements of your plan:

1. **Vision.** This is your why. Why are you doing what you do? It refers to the strategic-planning-level, big-picture vision of your enterprise. What do you see the world or community doing because of your idea? What do you want it to look like? As an example, Janine shared she worked with a doctor who wanted to focus her practice on women's health, in particular (but not limited to) rural menopausal women. The result was three words, 'Happy, healthy women,' which encapsulated perfectly the passion and vision for what her business is about.

   Janine advises that less is more when it comes to vision statements. 'Long-winded vision statements are less likely to have buy-in from other people,' she says. A short, clear statement (e.g. Rotary's 'A World Without Polio') tells everyone what your vision and aim is.

2. **Mission statement.** The mission statement is the 'how' of your business. In other words, the mission statement explains how you are going to implement your vision. For instance, working with Janine, I identified that my vision for *The Joyful Business Club* is 'Women shining at their full potential'. The accompanying mission statement is '*The Joyful Business Club* champions a vibrant, global community of agile businesswomen through mentoring, knowledge, networking, training and finances'.

3. **Values.** Any business startup needs to understand its values. And as discussed in Chapter 1, it's important to be clear on your values. It becomes even more important when you start bringing people into the business—whether it's customers, staff or suppliers. If they don't fit with your values, it's likely to cause challenges.

   In my case, for instance, I am committed to diversity, inclusion and sustainability, and have a zero-tolerance approach to bullying. The publication I was writing for last year didn't align with these values. If I had continued to write for them on their terms, a key risk was that my tribe could have abandoned me as I was not being authentic to my values.

4. **Objectives.** Objectives refer to the core, big-picture, achievable concepts. 'Without objectives, you start writing lists and the lists get bigger and bigger and longer and longer and you just get overwhelmed, feel you can't achieve it all and walk away from your business,' advises Janine. 'Instead, ask what are my big picture objectives? What do I want to achieve in twelve months? Or longer?'

DRAFTING A DETAILED BUSINESS PLAN

How do you go from writing a plan on a page to a slicker and fuller professional business plan? And how do you ensure it's a document that guides and helps your business rather than just something you set and forget?

> *My plan is unfolding in line with my vision,*
> *values and objectives.*

As mentioned previously, there are thousands of business plan templates on the internet—most for free. And I have developed a short and easy-to-use template. There is also an Australian Government-produced business plan, available for free at business.gov.au.

The template available at business.gov.au may seem daunting at first. It is nineteen pages in length and there is space to add additional supporting information (such as balance sheet forecasts, market research and even staff résumés). For a startup newbie, some of the fields in the template can seem confronting. How are you going to know what your financials are or what your organisational structure is when you are a solopreneur with a good idea?

It's important to note that this plan is just a template, and it can be customised. If you want it to truly reflect your business and what it stands for, it's a good idea to change it to suit your circumstances. And if you find the size of this business plan daunting, you can start with a lean business plan template, also available at business.gov.au.

Bec McFarland says she routinely adapts the stock-standard template. 'There are some areas of the template I suggest you just go and put in the bin,' she says. For instance, she doesn't like focusing on competition and considers spending time analysing competitors as less time spent on her own business (we talk more about competitors and collaborators in Chapter 8). She has also modified her business plan to include language on diversity and inclusion.

UPDATING YOUR PLAN

For your plan to be effective, it's important to review it regularly. A beautifully written plan is useless unless you put it into action. An effective business plan is much more than a tick-the-box document that hides somewhere on your computer; it's a living plan that needs to be reviewed and updated regularly.

It's also likely that, despite all of your planning, your plan might not work. There might be something key missing, such as the revenue model not being right or the product not suiting your market. Or maybe, despite all your planning and testing, customers just don't want to buy the product or service.

On this, Napoleon Hill has some good advice: 'If the first plan which you adopt does not work successfully, replace it with a new plan, if this new plan fails to work, replace it, in turn with still another, and so on, until you find a plan which DOES WORK. [8]

'The most intelligent man living cannot succeed in accumulating money—nor in any other undertaking—without plans which are practical and workable. Just keep this fact in mind, and remember when your plans fail, that temporary defeat is not permanent failure. It may only mean that your plans have not been sound. Build other plans. Start all over again.'

And next time, you will be more familiar with the planning process.

GOVERNMENT PROGRAMS

There are several Australian and State or Territory Government programs that can support you through the development and growth of your business. Many are low cost or free.

Websites you can search for information about possible schemes include:

- business.gov.au
- nsw.gov.au
- vic.gov.au
- act.gov.au/business

MY BUSINESS PLAN

I have developed a template for my business planning purposes, which is a rough amalgam of the 'plan on a page' and the longer business.gov. au template. To download a free copy of the template, visit my website at joyfulbusiness.club.

EXERCISES

1.

Are you putting off starting a side hustle or something in your business because it isn't perfect yet? If so, what are you holding off doing?

2.

What is the vision for your business?
What is the big-picture issue that motivates you?

3.

How are you going to implement your business? List a few ways you plan to bring your vision to life. (i.e. Combating climate change could be broken down into a mission for encouraging people to compost.)

4.

What do you want to achieve over the next twelve months?

5.

What do you want to achieve this month?

6.

What are your priorities for this week?

4

BRANDING
AND LOGOS

When you're in the early throes of starting a business, or thinking about starting a business, one of the most exciting things is envisaging the branding. This is often one of the biggest and most important business decisions you will make, and one that will define how people see you and your business.

But it's also one where people often get it wrong.

The good news is that you don't have to spend a fortune to nail your branding. The other good news is that branding can be changed or updated—although not without cost.

In this chapter, I focus on some of the steps that will help you think strategically about your business and identify your brand story.

THE ACCIDENTAL BRAND

Some people have a very clear vision of what their business will be like from the get-go. They sit down and write business plans and strategic visions and their businesses unfold to a T. But as we saw in the last chapter, they are rare.

Instead, many of us start from an imperfect-action premise of trying a bit of this and that. We lean into one thing or another, and our business grows and forms. This is especially the case for female entrepreneurs, many of whom might start with a small on-the-side business while balancing babies, and then scale it up when they are at a different stage of life.

An example of an entrepreneur whose business has chameleoned is Bec Cuzzillo. Bec started out selling stylish essential-oil-scented soy candles. She still sells candles, but after having her first child, Bec decided to focus more on group coaching, including her Spiritual Business Mistressmind program aimed at supporting spiritual women to build and scale their business. She is now also a podcaster.

My book and podcast, both named *The Joyful Frugalista*, also evolved along an unplanned path. In 2010, I started blogging about recipes and life in Taiwan (I lived in Taipei from 2010 to 2014) under the name *Taiwanxifu*. Then in 2013, I started a side blog called *The Weekend Parent*, which was about being a career-focused person who struggled to relate to her kids on the weekend. After my family and I returned to Australia, I became a single parent and needed to be super careful with my money. I started writing about frugal tips and recipes and renamed the blog *MsFrugal Ears*. I was later offered a book deal and the publisher came up with the title *The Joyful Frugalista*. They also suggested I do a rebrand to fit.

I loved the new name and branding. The book cover is a distinctive bright pink with blue and gold. I would never have come up with *The Joyful Frugalista* in that beautiful form back in 2015 when I started writing about frugal living (nor earlier when I was blogging in Taiwan). But now that I have that brand, I've ensured the branding for its sister entities—*The Joyful Business Club* and *The Joyful Fashionista*—is consistent.

As we grow and our businesses grow and change, sometimes our businesses evolve without us even realising it. According to branding expert Litsa Barberoglou from Brandivine, a lot of businesses (especially female-led businesses) start as side hustles or grow from a small base and then expand into something else over time. Often, branding hasn't been the core driver; in the early days, it's more about sales. 'People focus on how they are going to get sales promoting themselves,' she says. 'And generally, they only start to think about their branding a couple of years later.'

BRANDING VERSUS LOGO

When people think of branding, they usually think about a logo. But branding is much broader than a logo. A logo is a visual representation of your brand. It is an important part of your business identity. When you see the McDonald's golden arches, the Nike swoosh, the Mercedes-Benz emblem or the red-and-white Coca-Cola can, you know exactly what the product is and what it stands for. (Or at least, you trust that it will deliver what it promises.) I'll talk about logos later in this chapter.

But before you start designing your logo, you need to do some deep strategic thinking on what your business is about. What is your brand? And what does it stand for? Lista Barberoglou cautions that often people go out and start getting excited about pretty colours, fonts and graphics without knowing what their brand is about. 'If you haven't defined your brand, how can you get the optimal visual representation of it?' she says.

I can relate to this. I like ideas and possibilities, and there have been so many times I've started down the road of coming up with a cool name for a business and thought about colour schemes and the look and feel. I've even created Facebook pages and websites. I find it fun to think about this: it's kind of like having a new doll or toy and finding a name. But the journey to a brand is much more than this initial stage of thinking about names. While you do need to listen to your intuition about the colours, look and feel, it is important to go even deeper to understand your brand.

> *I trust my intuition to guide me to the right colour, look and feel to represent my business.*

WHY YOUR 'WHY' IS YOUR BRAND STORY

To get to understand what a brand is about, Litsa Barberoglou says she goes through a process of asking her clients a series of questions about their business. She does this to uncover what a business is really, truly about; it's not always obvious.

Litsa suggests people starting a business ask themselves a range of deep, probing questions, including:

- What does my brand stand for?
- Who am I?
- What story am I trying to tell my potential customers?
- Why do I do what I do?
- What is my brand purpose?
- How do I express what my business is about in a concise and connected way?

According to Litsa, a brand identity goes deeper than a goal of just making money. For instance, a business might be a cleaning company—but beyond cleaning, it has a core purpose. Litsa, therefore, asks her clients why they are involved specifically in a particular endeavour. 'I like to softly probe my clients, and as I start to probe, sometimes we begin to understand that the reason people are doing this particular thing is that they have a deeply held passion, or a heartfelt belief or something that they're committed to emotionally,' she says.

She says she often has moments with her clients when she gets goosebumps after hearing the answers they come up with. 'OMG, sometimes when I hear what my clients have shared with me it is so deeply personal and I feel humbled that they have shared it,' she says.

That then is the brand story. It's the 'why'—it's the essence of the business and becomes the narrative that drives the brand development.

> *I know who I am, and I am open to sharing my story.*

We are often intrigued to learn why a founder started a business or startup. We want to know the backstory of the single mum who invented a product to make caring for young children easier, the teenager who invented something in Mum and Dad's garage, and the entrepreneur in their fifties or sixties who decided to embark on a new venture while others were retiring. When I look at a website for a product, I will usually go straight to the 'About' page. Journalists also love the personal story and will highlight that more than the product in news stories.

PERCEPTION AND TRUST

Aranka Nolan from Einstein Marketing Group likens the process of developing a brand to getting ready to go out on a date. 'There are two parties coming together with expectations,' says Aranka. 'If you are going on a date, you will likely put a lot of effort into dressing to convey the right image about you. And just like a date, in your business, you need to put in the work to ensure that people get the right first impression of your brand.'

If you think about it, when you go out on a date with someone, you are conscious of the image you want to convey. You want them to think the best about you—you want to appear attractive, interesting, successful, intelligent, caring, stylish or whatever fits your values. They say that a book shouldn't be judged by its cover, but we judge people on first impressions all the time. The same is true of brands.

CASE STUDY
Thankyou

Have you ever been in someone's bathroom and seen a bottle of Thankyou handwash? How did that change what you thought about your host (or the business you were at)?

I first saw a bottle of Thankyou handwash at a party for a friend's son. I didn't know anything about the company, but I immediately understood they wanted to achieve something more than just selling a bottle of handwash. The bottle looked nice (perhaps not coincidentally like the high-end Aesop brand), the product felt good when I lathered it up, and it had a whole hip and good-karma vibe to it. More than anything, I remember thinking What nice people of my hosts.

Fast forward and I now use Thankyou handwash in my home and in my Airbnb. Somewhat cheekily, I want people to know that I'm committed to a values-based life—and by connection, think that I'm a good person and a good host. It's a brand I want not just in my house, but in my home.

Thankyou was founded in 2008 by a group of university students.[9] It produces body care and food items—including items for babies—with profits going to fund hygiene, sanitation and food-security programs. While they initially started with Thankyou Water, they moved away from this for environmental reasons. They (and their customers) actively lobbied Coles and Woolworths to stock their products.

In August 2013, media reports revealed that thirty per cent of Thankyou's profits were going to Samaritan's Purse, an evangelical Christian organisation that was not a signatory to the Australian Council for International Development's Code of Conduct. Thankyou has since stopped supporting this organisation.[10]

To date, Thankyou has raised over $17 million for its

impact partners, who work to eradicate poverty. In October 2020, Thankyou invited global brands, including P&G and Unilever, to collaborate to end poverty through its campaign No Small Plan.[11]

Continuing with the going-on-a-date analogy, you probably wouldn't even agree to a face-to-face meeting with someone unless there was a certain degree of trust. You would probably have read their profile, looked at their photo, chatted with them online, and maybe even checked out their LinkedIn profile before you agreed to meet them in person. So just like with a date, there is a lot of trust building that needs to happen, and often this happens before someone makes a purchase.

With a brand, the aim is to create a climate of trust so people don't just want to go on a first date with you—but rather, want an ongoing relationship. Once you've defined your purpose and you're consistent with how you communicate that, it is important to cement the fundamentals of trust.

WHAT'S THE BIG DEAL BETWEEN BRANDING AND TRUST?

Just think of the brand of products you use: the car you drive, the toothbrush you use, the products you use to wash a baby with, what you feed your kids for breakfast, or the food you feed your furbaby. All of these products were chosen based on trust; you want the very best not just for yourself, but for those you care about.

Litsa Barberoglou says brand trust is more than just about increasing sales: research points to the fact that when you are trusted as an entity, your clients are more loyal to you, your staff are more engaged, and you get better referrals. Earning true trust is more than just coming up with a catchy branding statement. Once trust is embedded in your business, you can reap a range of benefits.

2021 TRUSTED BRANDS AUSTRALIA WINNERS

The following are some of the winners of the 2021 Trusted Brands awards.[12]

Australian Iconic Brand	Bunnings Warehouse
Bank of the Year	Bendigo Bank
Vacuum Cleaners	Dyson
Supermarkets	Woolworths
Tea	Twinings
Pain Relief	Panadol
Milk	Dairy Farmers
Household Cleaning Products	Dettol
Funeral Insurance	Suncorp
Fabric Softener/Conditioner	Comfort
Dishwashing Liquid	Morning Fresh
Cheese	Bega Cheese
Cars	Toyota
Breakfast Food	Weet-Bix

How many of these brands do you use? Have you ever stopped to consider why you trust the brands you consistently use? What type of messaging and work have they done to get you to trust them?

Is Twinings the best tea? It's got a royal seal of approval. But a few years ago, a friend posted to Colombo gifted me a box of Ceylon loose-leaf tea. It was the nicest Earl Grey tea I have ever tasted. Why do we pay top dollar for Twinings rather than other tea? There are many reasons, but a big part of it is the label and the assurance that it is a quality tea. (And yes, I do drink Twinings as well.)

And what about breakfast cereals? Are manufactured cereals better than homemade oats? While some are better than others, from a nutritional point of view, it's not always the case. Would you pay fifty dollars for a box of cereal? According to some reports, at one point, that's what Chinese consumers were paying for a box of Weet-Bix.[13] Thankfully, I don't need to pay that to keep my Weet-Bix-eating kids happy. (Thankfully also, they are happy with a generic version).

Consciously or not, we make decisions about brands based on trust—especially when it comes to our families.

BRANDING AND COMPANY CULTURE

Having a good brand aligned with your brand story (and values) is more than just a sales gimmick. It is more powerful than click funnels. It is more powerful than hiring media stars to spruik your product. And it's one of the most powerful tools you have to motivate and retain the best possible employees.

According to Litsa Barberoglou, she once had a less-than-positive experience interacting with a staff member from a longstanding client. She was surprised; the staff member didn't seem to fit with the values of her client. It turned out that other employees also noticed this person was not a good cultural fit and threatened to resign en masse if that person continued to work there.

CASE STUDY
Zappos

Zappos sells shoes and clothing. It is an independent subsidiary of Amazon and hires nearly 1,300 employees. The company hires for cultural fit, with one of its core values to 'create fun and a little weirdness'. The company actively recruits staff around the values of fun, passion and personality, and is committed to customer service. During recruitment, Zappos even asks interviewees to rank how 'weird' they are. It's a company that values individuality.[14]

Zappos has a unique way of ensuring future employees are a good cultural fit for its brand. If an applicant is offered an interview and doesn't live locally, the company sends a van to the airport to pick them up. It's not just a convenience, or even a nice gesture, but an integral part of the interview process. During the commute, the van driver observes the applicants. And after a full day of recruitment activities, the van driver gets to give their opinion on whether to make a job offer.

In 2013, CEO Tony Hsieh told The Wall Street Journal that 'it doesn't matter how well the day of interviews went, if our shuttle driver wasn't treated well, then we won't hire that person.'[15]

BRANDING MISTAKES

Litsa Barberoglou says one of the worst mistakes is to create a cool, hipster brand that isn't aligned with who you are—and that no one understands. She cautions this creates barriers for potential customers, as they can't understand what the brand is about.

This is especially the case where the 'cool' brand uses unusual combinations of letters and numbers in its name or seeks to look street-art trendy without any explanation, and where the name has no obvious link to the business purpose. SeedInvest is a crowdfunding platform that facilitates startup investments. From the name, you can easily get a sense of what the company is about. In comparison, what does unu say about its business? It's a German e-scooter manufacturer, but its name doesn't easily communicate what it does (at least not in Australia).

I admit I thought it was just me who felt old and uncool with brands that were trying to be uber hipster. I feel like I don't belong, that they have created a super-cool-kids club and I'm the geeky boomer who isn't party to the in-joke. I don't want to spend my dollars on supporting a brand that makes me feel like I'm on the outer.

Have you ever felt like that with a brand? How could you prevent your brand from creating unwitting barriers?

> *My brand is inclusive and I attract clients and*
> *employees aligned with my brand values.*

The other big mistake is rushing out to develop a cheap logo before thinking about the brand story. Many startups will go out and develop a logo by themselves on an application like Canva or Fiverr. It's not necessarily bad. I've seen a few good examples where this has worked. And when you're in the rush of excitement about a new business venture, it's natural to start thinking about names and logos.

But there are many examples of where the logos are just ordinary (or worse, don't represent the brand and are just cookie-cutter).

According to Litsa, you will never get the branding right the first time round—it will be an evolution. The secret is to first put some thought into what your brand is all about. 'Start thinking about your business before designing a logo. If I was talking to someone about the purpose of my business, what would I say?' she says. 'What would you want to be known about as a business?'

BRAND DIFFERENTIATION

In developing your brand, you also need to develop something unique to you. If you are clear about your brand story, you are likely developing something authentic and unique. Just trying to be different and not be something else isn't the answer; you need to be you.

Litsa Barberoglou recommends examining how your brand will protect you against potential threats. 'What is it that makes you different that isn't going to mean you are susceptible to things like a price war?' she says. 'How will you differentiate yourself from your competitors?'

In everything I do, I have competitors who are doing similar things—including in my community. It's easy to get freaked out in the beginning and lose your nerve. How can you compete with others doing the same? The reality is your offering is *not the same*. Unless you are consciously seeking to knock off other people's ideas (which I suggest is not an ethical strategy, nor something that will bring you long-term success), your offering will be unique. (More about this in Chapter 8.)

For instance, many people write about personal finance and there are many podcasts on the topic. What new insights could I possibly offer? I didn't let this stop me from writing *The Joyful Frugalista* (nor from starting a podcast). My book often resonates with a gen X audience, especially with women who have gone through a hardship, such as a separation, or who are doing well in their professional lives but yearn for financial freedom. It also appeals to women and men who want to embrace sustainability and long-term wealth creation.

My book isn't for everyone; young men, for instance, often prefer strategies and steps to obtain big-figure wealth over a book with a bright-pink cover. They probably don't want to read something written by someone who looks and sounds like their mother. And I get it. While they are welcome to read my book and listen to my podcast, they aren't my target market and I don't change my style to focus on them.

REBRANDING

Sometimes, as your business grows, develops and changes, the branding needs an update. Litsa Barberoglou spent seven years in a business that produced printed clothing, promotional material and other merchandise. When she left that to set up a new business in branding and marketing, she wondered whether to continue using the same branding. On advice from a friend, she ditched the original branding and created something new; it was a new business and needed a new look.

Sometimes people can become emotionally attached to branding. Often, they have created the branding—especially the logo—themselves and have had it for a long time. Their brand identity from the 1990s might not match where it is in the world today. For instance, think about how different life was before smartphones. Does your brand speak to a digitally aware audience? Does it need updating?

Sometimes a brand needs to change because of negative media that has undermined trust in the brand. For instance, following widespread negative media in Australia over the AstraZeneca brand of the COVID-19 vaccine, it has rebranded to become Vaxzevria.[16] Same product, different name.

But according to Aranka Nolan, negative media doesn't necessarily spell the death of a brand. She has worked with companies who have needed to work hard to regain trust after major problems or issues. 'It is possible to regain trust,' she says. 'But it does require extraordinary effort and strong leadership.'

LOGO

With all this discussion about creating a compelling brand story, you could be forgiven for thinking that a logo is unimportant. Not so. A logo is the visual representation of your brand. It is what people see when they look at you as a business. And as around seventy per cent of people prefer to communicate visually, it is an important way to send a distinctive message about your company.

Think about some brands you know. Where do you bank? What apps do you use? What fast-food restaurants have you eaten at (or refuse to eat at)? Where do you stop for petrol? What clothing do you like to wear? What about footwear?

What are their logos? How recognisable are they? When you see the logo, do you know what the company is? And if so, do you trust it?

Logos are an essential part of building a business brand. In the long run, a well-thought-out and distinctive logo will be one of the best investments for your business. A logo is how customers will know that your product or service is from your company. Symbols are important, and that's why big companies invest in logo development.

CASE STUDY
Nike Swoosh

Look at any Nike product and you will see the distinctive Swoosh logo—and it will bring the 'Just do it' motto to mind. The logo, which suggests movement, also suggests wings; Nike is the name of the winged Greek goddess of victory.

The Nike Swoosh was designed in 1971 by graphic design student Carolyn Davidson, who received $35 for her work. One of the Nike founders, Phil Knight, was an associate professor at Portland State University where Carolyn was studying. He knew Carolyn and knew she needed money to take oil painting classes. He offered her the two-dollars-an-hour job so that she could earn a bit of extra income. Carolyn spent seventeen and a half hours on the job, using tissue paper to mock up the design on the side of shoes to see how the logo looked.

The founders didn't love the design at first—in fact, reports are they didn't like it—but due to production deadlines, chose the one they felt was the 'least awful'. By the 1980s, it was clear the Swoosh was a winner. Nike threw Carolyn a large thank-you party and gifted her a Nike ring. Carolyn reportedly has over a million dollars in Nike stock options, and the logo's success has benefited her private freelancing career.[17]

According to Litsa Baberoglou, once a brand story is created and defined, creating your logo and marketing materials then becomes easy. This is why getting your values and brand story right first, before thinking about colours and fonts, will make it easier.

Litsa likens the process to designing and building a new house. Before you start stacking bricks, it's best to do a lot of design work to decide what you want your house to look like. In most cases, people will get an architect to draw up plans based on what they want their house to look like (and how they plan to use it). An inner-city apartment block, for instance, will look quite different from a family home on acreage. If the property is using an interior designer, they will also brief their designer on what they want.

The same happens with logo design. If you have a skilled and professional graphic designer doing your logo development work, they won't just rush in and create something in hot pink for you. First, they will ask detailed questions about what your brand is about. What product or service does it sell? What is the target demographic? What are the values? What does the logo need to convey?

Litsa says that if you are not briefing a graphic designer properly, you aren't allowing them to show their skill set. You need to be able to communicate how you want to look, sound, think and speak to ensure that your logo is consistent. If the end logo is incongruous with your vision, you are not going to be able to maximise the opportunities for your brand. One of the risks with a low-cost solution is that you will end up with a template logo that won't necessarily fit your brand.

I remember early on getting a logo developed from Fiverr for what became *The Joyful Frugalista*. At that time, the website was called *Ms Frugal Ears*. I didn't love the logo I had developed. It didn't look unique, and the use of dollar signs made it look cheap. I used it for a while, but I was happy when the name and look of the website changed to *The Joyful Frugalista*.

In contrast, when graphic designer Lib Ferreira designed the logos for *The Joyful Business Club* and *The Joyful Fashionista*, we had a long chat. After that, I filled in surveys. It was an interesting process and it forced me to think deeply about what I was trying to achieve. Both businesses were aimed at empowering women, but in different ways. Abundance and inclusivity were also important values, as was sustainability.

Lib nailed it in the first design for *The Joyful Business Club*. I felt the navy background and gold coins were striking. It is stylish and suggests manifesting big abundance and universal possibilities, without needing to state it in a tacky way. I feel it speaks to women who want to shine like a star in the sky and support other women as they shine in their glory.

The logo for *The Joyful Fashionista* is even more stylish and distinctive. But it was harder to get it right. Lib and I had several discussions, and she tweaked many designs. The underlying issue is that fashion can be contentious. I feel fashion has traditionally been framed as the domain of the perfect—the young, the thin, the tall, the Caucasian and the rich. I wanted an image that celebrated inclusivity and sustainability. I also saw my target market as slightly older, with few having perfect body shapes. But I still wanted it to be stylish and to show how second-hand clothing is sustainable, while also celebrating beauty and individuality. I wanted every woman, whatever her budget, to feel like an empress in her new (second-hand) clothes.

Navigating these themes in a brand story was no easy task, but Lib rose to the occasion. The result is a logo that looks beautiful and stylish, but hints at curves. The look and feel of this brand are also consistent with that of *The Joyful Business Club* and *The Joyful Frugalista* via the use of coins, and harks back to *The Joyful Frugalista* with reference to the dress.

ELEMENTS OF AN EFFECTIVE BRAND STRATEGY

Branding is so much more than a logo. In terms of the visual design elements, it refers to everything you can see: the logo, print material, advertising, social media graphics, presentations, website, packaging and photography.

According to Lib Ferreira, the way you use your branding is important. She suggests the following tips for maximising your brand potential.

1. **Be professional.** Appearances are everything when it comes to successful branding. People notice what you look like. And if you don't look professional, then people can perceive that you lack credibility and they might not trust your business. To successfully sell professional services and quality products, you need to look professional to avoid losing potential customers or clients.

2. **Be unique.** Your business needs to stand out in a highly competitive, over-saturated market. One of the best ways to do this is to be unique. Don't follow current trends, and don't just copy what your main competitor is doing. You also need to ensure you do not run into any legal issues regarding copyright or plagiarism. Check your business name on the ASIC's business name register to ensure it is not common in your industry. If you are using an image or graphic, another tip is to check there is nothing similar being used (or overused) by doing a reverse image search on Google.

3. **KISS—Keep it simple, stupid.** In design, simple is best. A complicated logo could fail if your potential customers can't read the name of your business. Simple logos are also more versatile, which means you do not run into issues when trying to design for different sizes and formats. Simple designs are also

quick and easy to recognise. People's attention spans are short and getting shorter, and you need to be able to achieve quick recognition to capture your audience.

4. **Be consistent.** It is important to use the same colours, fonts, and style of images consistently across all your branding. A good graphic designer will provide you with a brand kit that includes things like the hex codes for the colours that are used in your design. Everything needs to look the same across all your communication channels to avoid confusion by your client and increase the awareness of your business.

EXERCISES

1.

What does my brand stand for?

2.

Who am I?

3.

What story am I trying to tell my potential
customers?

4.

Why do I do what I do?

5.

What is my brand purpose?

6.

How do I describe my business or startup in
a concise and connected way?

7.

Has my company evolved or changed?
And if so, is my brand still consistent?

8.

What does my logo say about my brand?

9.

Am I using my brand identity consistently across
all platforms (social media, newsletters, Powerpoint
presentations, etc.)?

5
NETWORKING

In the first few months after I left work, I felt like I had to work super-long hours to prove myself. I spent hours crouched un-ergonomically over my home computer, answering emails efficiently, writing copy and wanting to be seen to be busy, busy, busy. For some reason, I wanted to prove that I was even more effective working from home and establishing my new business than when I had been at work full time.

And then my friend Misty Henkel invited me to a networking event.

I knew Misty through my Zonta club, and she was insistent that I attend a breakfast networking event. Misty, aka the networking and sales queen, is the author of *Overcoming Obscurity: How to get noticed in the marketplace so that you can make more money*. She is famous in Canberra (and increasingly, nationally and even internationally) and anyone who has ever been to a networking event knows her. Just go to a networking event and ask 'Hey, have you met Misty?' and invariably people will know her. When Misty invites you to a networking event, she won't take no for an answer.

While I had been to many networking events in the past, I wasn't sure how it would go. At other events, I had felt like a bit of a fraud as I wasn't *yet* a real business owner. I had an ABN, I'd written a book, and I was doing freelance writing, but that was about all. I didn't have staff, nor was I earning a big income.

Misty told me to be at a cafe at 6.45 am on Thursday. 'Make sure you come with at least thirty business cards,' she said. But what she forgot to tell me was that I would need to stand up in front of a room of strangers and deliver a thirty-second pitch.

At my first meeting, we went around the room and people stood up and delivered their pitches in brisk procession—there were over thirty of us. One of the members recorded each pitch. Everyone seemed professional and confident in front of the camera. There were so many businesses—everything from search-engine optimisation (SEO) support to government-backed training courses and even other authors. Everyone had a pitch about what they did. Would I even be accepted in this group? To be honest, I was barely awake and not feeling glam.

I was accepted into that group—and in other networking groups as well. Many of those people I met on the first morning have since become not only business acquaintances, but also close friends.

> *I belong.*

But it didn't happen overnight, and it wasn't instantaneous. You may go to a networking group for the first time, walk away and think *Well, that was a bit of a waste—I didn't even sell anything!* But over time, you will turbocharge your business by knowing the right people at the right time to help you.

WHY NETWORK?

Networking has been one of the best things I have done to propel my businesses forward since leaving work. I've sold books, training courses and coaching spots, and gained podcasting guests and people to interview for Facebook Lives. Many of the people I have met have mentored me in business, and unsurprisingly, many of them also feature in this book. Many of them will buy this book—some may buy it before it has even been published—and leave glowing reviews and tell other people to buy it. I know this to be true because I do this for other people in the group, and others do it for me.

For me, networking is not about what I have sold or gained in my business so much as the connections that I make. Looking back on nearly two years of networking, the results are amazing. Using my networking contacts, I sold an investment property, had business logos designed, was mentored in website design and SEO, enjoyed massages, learned how to use Canva, connected with business coaches and mastermind groups, scored my first podcast sponsor, and found a physio to help my son recover from a concussion.

And that's not even half of it. People think I have a big black book of contacts, and even friends who don't network ask me if I can recommend people with expertise in different areas. Often, I will know just the person. This is the power of networking.

It's not surprising that networking is so successful, because relationships form the basis of doing business. Successful businesses build trust, and trust comes through relationships with people.

THE CHINESE ART OF GUANXI

In Chinese culture, relationships are so valued that there is a specific term—*guanxi* (关系). Guanxi occurs when there is a high level of mutual trust, and it usually develops over time. When you have guanxi with someone, you have a special relationship with them. They will often happily provide favours, such as discounts on goods or services, or go a step extra. They might get you a ticket to a sold-out event or organise a private visit to a doctor (and accompany you). They will go the extra mile because you have guanxi with them. It's a two-way street and you are expected to reciprocate. More likely, you would have invested in the relationship before the favour was asked, which is how you built that guanxi in the first place. If not, you will consider it an honour to pay it back when the opportunity arises.

While guanxi has a specific role in Chinese business culture, it's not so dissimilar to doing business in Australia. For instance, if you know a tradie well, they are likely to offer you 'mates rates'—or at least prioritise your work. And you can trust that they will do a good job. After all, you are not just any customer; you're a mate. And of course, you are going to tell all of your friends about what a fabulous job your tradie mate has done and recommend them to many other people. This is the type of relationship you can build through networking, and this is a good example of why networking matters.

As outlined above, there is no question that my business (and me personally) has benefited from networking. But it is so much more than outcomes. During those dark COVID lockdown days, the weekly Zoom networking meetings were what kept me afloat with the glimmer of successful business emerging after the doom and gloom. I realised that my networking groups had become my support network, a grouping that kept me focused and alive.

When you are starting out, one of the issues is that people in your immediate orbit (e.g. family and friends) might not get where you are coming from. They don't understand the fears you face about venturing into new territory, nor can they mentor or help you. They haven't been there. Other business owners understand your journey, and in my experience, are generally willing to help and support you. I realised that many of my networking contacts had become more than just business cards; they had morphed into lifelong friendships.

NETWORKING IS NOT DIRTY

In one of my mastermind groups, I shared a *Harvard Business Review* article that discusses research about how many people feel dirty when networking.[18]

We need to change this mindset. Networking is much deeper than self-promotion (and in fact, one-sided self-promotion is rarely effective in any case).

Over a decade ago, I worked in a role that involved national security preparedness. We had regular meetings with stakeholders and conducted exercises that were designed to help everyone understand the roles and responsibilities of different departments and agencies. If a major national-security event occurred, you needed to know who to call—and it helped if you had a relationship with them before something blew up.

Translate that into your business. How can you effectively grow your business if you don't know who to trust to build your website? Give you marketing advice? Design your logo? Refer clients to you? Fix your computer if it gets hacked?

You might know who to call if you have a business emergency or need specialist help. And you might just be there to help someone else on their journey at the right time. Being an intuitive person, I like to feel that through networking I am often connected with the right people at the time I need them. Just as I need to take the next step with my business, someone appears to help me.

> *My business attracts the right people at the right time.*

You are most likely building your business because it is something you are passionate about. You need to network so that you can share your passion with others. It's not selfish; you have a gift to give and it would be more selfish not to offer it. Know that networking is about building connections so that you can help others as well as yourself.

TIPS TO OVERCOME NETWORKING ANXIETY

Recently, a friend said to me, 'I know I need to network, but I feel so anxious doing it. It doesn't feel natural to promote myself in this way. What's the secret?'

I paused and thought about this for a bit. I guess the real secret for me is that I *like* people and I *enjoy* meeting them. I'm a self-identified extrovert, and I get my energy from being around other people.

It's perhaps hard to believe that when I was at school, I was a bit of a social misfit. I didn't have many friends. It's not that people didn't like me; individually I had some good conversations, but in a group setting, I didn't know how to relate to others or make conversation. I found myself talking too much about myself and, in my nervousness, talking over others. I guess I was trying to be entertaining, and in the process behaved like a performing clown rather than connecting. Over time, I worked on improving my interpersonal skills and I can now say that I find networking fun and rewarding.

I started going to Rotary meetings with my ex-husband. Rotarians are good at networking; they do it every week. I remember walking into a room and feeling a bit daunted, but the people at my table were professional and polite. I found myself easily engaged in conversations with (mostly) older and successful people, who appeared to be genuinely fascinated by what I had to say. Looking back, the thing I remember is them asking lots of questions about me and actively listening to what I had to say. This new experience struck me and gave me the confidence to network effectively throughout my career and in business.

> *I enjoy meeting new people.*

Being an effective networker is so much more than just performing or broadcasting. These are some of my tips:

- **Get there early.** As someone who is naturally late, it takes a bit for me to reset my dial to get to a networking event early. But when I do, it makes a huge difference. I am calm, and have usually managed to get a good car park or navigate public transport. That means I am in a positive mood and more likely to make a good first impression. Who doesn't want to speak with someone relaxed, calm and happy rather than stressed and worried? As a bonus, arriving early allows me to meet some important people. I have learned that guest speakers, facilitators and high-performing regulars tend to get to networking events early and you are more likely to get an opportunity to talk to them before the event.

- **Research guest speakers beforehand.** Related to my point above, make sure you know a bit about the guest speaker or key personalities. You may be surprised how few people do. And I've been guilty of it.

One time, I was chatting to a lady in the women's toilets just before a course. 'Where do you work?' I asked. 'It's my course,' she answered. (She was and is the amazing Avril Henry, a keynote speaker, author and provocateur who is passionate about empowering women—and quite a celeb in her own right.)

Let that never happen to you. Yet, it does happen. Often. Only recently, I was in the elevator heading early to an event where I was one of two panellists. My CV and photo were in the promotion material. Yet the lady in the lift, with whom I was making small talk, had no idea at all who I was (even when I introduced myself, and even though she was booked to go to the event).

- **You don't need to meet everyone in the room.** Going to a networking event is not a competition to see how many business cards you can collect (I'll talk about business cards more in the next chapter). Effective networkers make genuine connections, and they don't try to speak to absolutely everyone at each event. Don't think there is something wrong with you if you don't connect with everyone. If you talk with two or three interesting people, that's fine. Even one if it's a genuine connection.

- **Ask about the other person.** Before you launch into talking about yourself, ask questions about the other person (just like the Rotarians did when I first met them, an experience that fifteen years on I still remember). I find people crave connection, and if you think about it, most people talk about themselves rather than ask about someone else. When you show interest in another person, that person is likely to glow in the opportunity to be heard.

Asking questions is effective. You don't have to be nosy or make someone feel like they are under police investigation. Just ask a few simple things like:

  - What brought you here today?
  - Have you been here before?
  - What is your business about?
  - How does that work?
  - What are the challenges in your industry at the moment?

- **Listening is the best form of communication.** Have you ever been to an event where you have met someone and you are talking, but they are gazing over your head, looking for someone more important or interesting than you? How did that make you feel? Or what about if someone talks over you when you speak? Active listening is a real skill. The best compliment you can give someone is to listen to what they are saying and to show from your body language that you are really, truly engaged.

- **Don't just spruik your wares.** Marg Lange from Marg Lange Change Agency says we buy from the people that we 'like, know and trust'. She says too many people go online or attend networking events, spruik their wares and urge people to buy their stuff—with zero awareness of what people have gone through (especially in a time of pandemics and natural disasters). 'Instead, we have to go back to the basics and start connecting and become a good conversationalist. We all love talking about ourselves. But we need to learn to stop putting the focus on us and put the focus on them,' she says.

- **Don't ask someone about their business or job unless they raise it.** Not all people have businesses or careers. Some are retired, some are looking after family, and some are looking to start. People can be super judgey about women in particular and what they do, and many women are sensitive to the seemingly innocuous question, 'What do you do?' Don't ask unless they refer to a career or business in conversation, and then ask open-ended questions to get them talking. If they are at a networking event, they are likely in business, but even so, don't assume.

- **Don't ask people where they are from.** If you are meeting in Australia, you can assume that most people are Australian or have a connection to Australia. If they start relating stories about 'when I grew up in Beijing' or 'what I miss about the food in Shanghai,' you can ask them about China. But for all you know, even though someone looks Chinese, they could be Japanese. Or Korean. Or a New Zealander. Or third-generation Australian. They've probably spent most of their lives trying to navigate identity politics and they may be over it. In my case, I happen to speak fluent Mandarin Chinese—but I don't go and start yabbering in Mandarin as soon as I meet someone who looks Asian. And yes, I've been caught out trying to speak Chinese with people who aren't Chinese, or who don't speak Mandarin, or whose families have been in Australia for several generations and it's always embarrassing.

- **Fake it until you make it.** Maybe you are just starting your business and you are not making a six-figure income. Maybe you don't even have any clients and you aren't making any money at all (yet). It doesn't matter. Put your professional 'I'm in business and I'm passionate about what I am doing' persona on, dress professionally, bring business cards and stand up and give a short pitch about what you are doing if asked. It's all about taking imperfect action and starting somewhere. Most businesspeople know what it's like to start. They still remember how raw it can feel. However, while it's okay to 'fake it' in terms of confidence, outright lying and misrepresenting your business is a different thing altogether.

CASE STUDY
Elizabeth Holmes

Elisabeth Holmes was the golden girl of entrepreneurship made female billionaire. Her company, Theranos, was once valued at USD9 billion. Holmes successfully attracted USD900 million in funding from investors including Rupert Murdoch and Larry Ellison.

Holmes claimed that she had developed a new blood-testing product that would revolutionise the healthcare industry by enabling testing using only a few drops of blood. No longer would people need to travel to a clinic for an uncomfortable blood test; now people could test from home using a patch.

The only problem was that the technology didn't work. In 2015, a Wall Street Journal investigation reported problems in Theranos's core blood-testing technology. In January 2022, jurors in a Californian court found Holmes guilty of conspiracy to commit fraud against investors and three charges of wire fraud.[19] The case has ignited debate about the 'fake it till you make it' motto, especially as this had implications for the health of people using the technology.

- **Use mirroring and labelling in conversation.** At networking events, especially when I don't know someone well (or I'm feeling shy and nervous), I like to employ a technique promulgated by former FBI lead hostage negotiator Chris Voss.[20] The mirroring tactic involves repeating keywords the other person used in conversation to show them that you are listening and have understood. For instance, if they ended by saying, 'I learnt a lot from starting my business,' you could respond with saying something like, 'Yes, starting a business is a real learning journey.' Labelling is about verbally acknowledging or summarising what someone was saying. For instance, you can use opening statements like, 'It seems like you have learnt a lot from your business journey.' I find these techniques are super effective signals that you are listening and engaged, and ensure that you need never fret about being without a witty conversation starter.

- **Have an elevator pitch ready.** If you were stuck in the elevator with someone famous, and they asked you what you did, how would you answer? It's important to always have an answer ready for when people ask you about yourself and your business. Practise your pitch in front of the mirror, with close friends, and at networking events. Ensure it sounds natural and that people can hear your passion for what you do. Also, make sure you vary it depending on who you speak to. For instance, if I meet someone who loves fashion, I'm more likely to just speak about *The Joyful Fashionista* than share my recipe for homemade baked beans.

- **Don't be scared to butt into a group.** Ever been to a networking function where you don't know anyone, and people are standing around in groups like they've been besties forever? You can break into a group; in fact, it's expected. The trick is to find the right group. Life coach Liz Fry Walton says at networking events there are closed and open circles. She advises that before seeking to join a conversation, scan the room to find an open circle, as they are the ones who are unconsciously going to welcome you in. As you enter the open circle, stand close by, listen for a bit and then join in. And after joining a group, if you see someone trying to join, do the polite thing and include them in the conversation. I usually smile and say, 'Hi, we were just talking about [XYZ].' That creates space for introduction and inclusion.

- **It is okay to mingle.** While turning a networking event into a speed-dating-style exercise is uncool (unless it is designed to be like that), it is acceptable to move around. After you have been chatting with someone (or a group), it is okay to leave—especially if someone new comes along and the conversation shifts. Just politely excuse yourself and say something like, 'It was lovely to meet you,' or 'I'm going to go and say hi to the host,' or 'I'm going to get another drink.'

- **Don't be greedy.** There's a saying that networking events are for work, and not for food and drink. Australian diplomat grads used to be taught to only have one thing in their hands at a time. A previous boss told me this as I was juggling a teacup and saucer and two pastries at an event at Australian Parliament House. She didn't approve. It can be hard to listen actively and swap business cards while you are juggling a handbag, a glass of champagne, and barbecue prawns on a stick. It can be even harder to do all of that while also taking food photos for Instagram (guilty). Keep in mind the impression you are sending. Be you and be authentic (nothing is going to stop me from taking foodie shots), but also focus on the people rather than the food and alcohol. Watch the alcohol, especially if there are people you want to impress.

- **Networking in COVID times.** In these pandemic times, it's especially important to follow public health guidelines. Don't touch or hug someone unless it is clear they are comfortable with you doing so. Saying, 'I don't care, I always do hugs,' isn't right; the other person could be immunocompromised or just not want their personal space violated. Do not go to an in-person networking event if you are unwell—passing on a lurgy (even if only the common cold) is not a good way to be remembered.

- **Networking online.** More and more networking events are moving online, and even after this pandemic, I expect the trend will continue. Networking online has its challenges—principally, it is not as easy to make the same sort of unscripted connections as it is when meeting someone in person. But it also has its advantages, including being able to meet people from throughout the world. A good way to network at online events is to keep your video on, look engaged and ask (or type) questions.

FIND YOUR NETWORKING TRIBE

Can't find a networking event? There are more opportunities than you might think.

I like Canberra Innovation Network's 'First Wednesday Connect' and 'Female Founders' series, and I also host events through *The Joyful Business Club* and have an online Facebook Live series. I love hearing about new networking forums—do stop by *The Joyful Business Club* to share.

YOUR LOCAL CHAMBER OF COMMERCE

Are you a member of your local chamber of commerce? If not, why not?

I had a great Facebook Live chat on *The Joyful Business Club* with Paul Boultwood, from the Corrimal Chamber of Commerce. You might be surprised by how many services your local chamber of commerce can offer you. Many chambers run networking events, and often they are an advocate for your business. Being connected and involved in your local chamber of commerce is a great way to build connections and know more about other businesses in your community.

LEARNING AND DEVELOPMENT COURSES

One of the best ways to meet people who share your passion and interests is to enrol in a training course. Not only will you learn some useful business, personal development or practical skills, but you could meet some amazing people in the process.

For instance, I recently did a sales course run by Nick McNaughton of Campus Plus at the Canberra Innovation Network. Not only was it an amazing (albeit scary) afternoon, but I ended up meeting a range of amazing people, including an Olympian entrepreneur, a government official working on entrepreneurship, and some successful startup founders.

DON'T FORGET THE BACKYARD BARBECUE!

Networking events are everywhere. Literally. Every time we interact with someone else, virtually or in person, we are networking. When I talk with other parents or with teachers at school, I am networking. When I go to a restaurant, I am networking. When I'm at a family Christmas party, I'm networking.

Think about it. There you are, sitting at a long Christmas lunch table with your family and extended family. Your niece's partner says, 'So, what do you do?' (My least favourite question.) Maybe you assume everyone knows about your business, but you might be surprised how little your family knows. Make sure you have an honest, non-braggy yet informative elevator pitch handy.

For instance, say you are a mortgage broker. You have a chat with your niece and her partner at Christmas lunch about the trends in the property market. Six months later, they buy a home together. Who better to turn to for mortgage advice than you, a trusted family member? And when her best friend buys a home of her dreams, your niece then recommends you and your circle grows.

Who would have thought you could network over turkey and ham?

As I type this, I've just organised a physio appointment for my youngest son (Audie) with my husband's daughter's partner (Mitch Barbara). I've had a few chats with Mitch about his previous sporting career and his interest in physio, so of course, I immediately thought to book in with him when Audie pulled a muscle at footie training.

And it's not just family events. Recently, I was at a barbecue event hosted by the coach of my youngest son's NRL team. I was a tad nervous as I'm a new footie mum and most of the time don't even really understand the rules. I also had an (as it turns out, incorrect) impression the kids in the team all went to the same school and knew each other.

I *could* have rocked up to the barbecue and spent the whole time stuck in a corner talking to my husband, or engaged in conversation only to talk about myself and my media appearances. Instead, I ended up learning a lot about two other footie mums. One managed a team in an organisation where I had been considering taking a job, and the other was doing some work to improve a retail precinct I visit regularly.

AFTER A NETWORKING EVENT

You've been to a networking event, you've met a few people, collected some cards (or details), then gone home or back to work. Going to a networking event in itself is great, but it's what comes afterwards that matters. How you follow up will make a world of difference. Otherwise, you might end up thinking that the event was pointless and that you didn't develop any deep *guanxi* relationships.

121

Meeting someone briefly at a networking event is good, getting their card or details is great, but following up with them individually for a 'one to one' (aka 121) meeting is even better. The 121 meeting is where you can get to know someone in more detail and explore opportunities for collaboration.

The 121 is not a social occasion, but it does help to share some personal anecdotes. For instance, after hearing Lib Ferreira's heartbreaking story of having a premature baby, when we met up for a virtual 121, I shared that my eldest son was born two months prematurely and wasn't expected to survive his first night. Those kinds of shared experiences say: *I hear you. I understand. I know why you are passionate about what you do.*

While being authentic and open is important for building genuine rapport and showing empathy, it would not, however, be appropriate to use a 121 with someone you don't yet know to vent about your husband, children, boss, neighbour or best friend. The person you are meeting with is someone you want to impress or suss out as a potential business connection. They are not your counsellor.

In the case of Lib, after cementing our shared preemie experiences, our conversation turned to the business reasons for the call: her graphic design and brand design work, my new business (*The Joyful Business Club*), the Live Your Best Life series she was working on with a fabulous mutual friend (Jeanene Kennedy from Winederlust), and ways in which our interests coincided. As I discussed in the last chapter, Lib went on to design new logos for *The Joyful Business Club* and *The Joyful Fashionista*, as well as flyers and Instagram tiles. I spoke at Live Your Best Life Series 2. I also invited Lib onto *The Joyful Business Club* to talk about brand design. And she's in this book!

While I've had some fantastic 121s, I've also (sadly) had several that were a waste of my time.

What makes a 121 good versus one that is bad?

In my experience, a 'bad' 121 occurs when someone requests it on their terms (i.e. at their preferred time and place), the purpose is unclear, and generally, the person wants to get something from you but is unwilling to give something in return. An example of a bad 121 is when I've driven the other side of town to meet someone for a long meeting, only to feel pressured to buy or promote their products—with no reciprocity or interest in what I do. Not only is it awkward for me to have to say no, but if they had taken the time to learn a bit about my business model, they would have known it wasn't going to be a good match.

I know I said that some 121s have been a waste of my time, but arguably *nothing* is a waste of time. While the meeting might not have been productive in terms of forming a genuine connection or relationship, and took time away from my business, I still came away with key learnings.

> *Learning comes in many forms.*

I also wish to add that there isn't an obligation to have a 121. If you meet someone at a networking event and you don't want to meet them, you don't have to. But if you follow the advice in this chapter, you are more likely to get a better outcome (or minimise the time spent in a bad one).

1. **Have a first short meeting.** If you have an online scheduling tool, it can be a great way to delineate a time. For instance, a meeting invite that says '30-minute Zoom chat' is likely going to last for thirty minutes. In my experience, a thirty-minute chat meeting rarely goes much longer than this. Contrast this with a casual 'let's catch up for coffee' invite. If you don't think the meeting will be that useful, with love, you can suggest that as your calendar is a bit tight, someone could first book in for a short online networking chat 'so that you can get to know each other a bit better first'. If you hit it off in a fifteen or thirty-minute chat, you can organise an in-person catch-up over lunch. You will be besties by then and it will be more enjoyable.

2. **Define the purpose.** When setting up the meeting, ask about the purpose of the meeting (especially if using a scheduling tool). For instance, the questions 'What do you hope to get out of the meeting?' and 'How could we collaborate?' help ensure the objectives for the meeting are clear upfront. If someone wants to recruit you for their sales pipeline and it's not something that you are interested in, you can prepare an answer early (or even say no to the meeting).

3. **Listen and connect.** Marg Lange says that, in a 121 meeting, it's important to listen and instil trust. It's not about going in and immediately trying to sell stuff. 'Once you have won over the trust barrier that they are not going to be sold to, everyone tends to just relax a bit,' she says. 'Now it's a conversation about what is going on for them and how you can be helpful.'

4. **Ask questions during the 121.** Liz Fry Walton is a creation coach and a mistress of networking. She has been involved in and facilitated networking meetings for many years. She and two friends also run the My Vibe women's networking group. She's had many years of networking experience, and during an educational spot, she shared her approach to 121s.

LIZ'S QUESTIONS
1. What do you do?
2. Why do you do what you do?
3. Why do you love what you do?
4. What are your challenges?
5. How can I support you now?

Liz also notes that question four is an opportunity to provide a referral.

REFERRALS

A key reason many people network is because of the referrals. We are all busy people, and want to feel like time away from our business is going to help it grow by bringing more business.

One of the best ways you can do this is through referrals. And giving referrals to other people is one of the best ways you can grow your own business.

It might be about connecting them to the right people. Marg Lange gives an example: 'Say I call you for a business meeting and you say that your fridge is not working and your whole day is going to shit. While I called you about selling my services, I stopped and listened to you and your problem, and then I took action by sending someone your way to fix the fridge right now.' Holding off on focusing on the sales call and instead helping fix a problem is one sure way to differentiate yourself as trustworthy.

Would many people help someone fix a fridge? Not many. But the ones who do generate trust and reliability. You can tell that they are listening to you and care about solving your problems. You are more likely to trust them with your business—and refer them to other people. 'The whole showing up differently strategy is about being helpful in ways that are outside what you do,' Lange says.

> *Be a connector rather than simply a connection.*

WARNING! WARNING!

A note of caution about referrals: just because someone refers someone to you, doesn't mean they are necessarily good. Sadly, I lost $23,300 after someone I trusted referred me to a website developer who didn't have the skills or competence to perform the task required, took seven months, and delivered a product that not only didn't have essential functionality but had two major security flaws. Not only was the developer referred by someone I knew well, but the Australian project manager and agent for the developer was part of my networking circle and someone I thought I liked and thought I could trust.

More recently, I've discovered there is someone who has been convicted of possessing child abuse material and someone else who has been bankrupt—twice—in one of the networking groups that had become like a second family to me.

It's important to always do your research. Check out people on LinkedIn, do a Google news search, and read online reviews. If it's a big job, always get references outside of a group.

And when referring someone's product or services, only do so if you have used their product or services and like what they do. If you can't evaluate in this way, make sure to tell the person you are making the referral to so they are aware. For instance, I recently referred someone in the public relations field. I was able to say, 'I know this person through [XYZ], in this context, and she seems to know what she's talking about, but I haven't worked with her on my own business.'

Further, just because someone has personally used someone's product or services, doesn't mean they will be the right fit for you and your business. Liz Fry Walton says that we are all different, and we all have different characters and some characters will blend with others. 'You might have used a plumber who did an excellent job for you, but then you refer them and that person doesn't have the same experience,' she says. Accordingly, she advises that even when you are referred to somebody, it is important to have a 121 to make sure you gel and build an understanding of what both parties want. 'We all have different filters and ways of seeing things,' she says.

FRUGALISTA TIP

If you attend a networking event, it is usually tax-deductible. This means you can reduce your taxable income by claiming the cost of networking breakfasts, training courses, and coffees when meeting to talk shop. Keep those receipts and claim at tax time. Even better, scan them on your phone and put them immediately into your online accounting platform. There is, however, a big difference between partying at your business's expense and genuine networking.

For further information, seek guidance from your accountant or check out the latest advice from the ATO (ato.gov.au).

EXERCISES

1.

Do some research into online and local networking events. When do they meet? What is their mission?

2.

Join The Joyful Business Club Facebook group.

3.

Challenge yourself to go to at least one event or networking group that you haven't been to before. Take a friend with you if you like, or even better, go it alone.

Follow up with a 121 meeting, especially with someone you would not normally think of as a good match for your business. Find out more about what they do and listen with an open mind.

6

BUSINESS CARDS
AND CRM

It is almost established knowledge that you need to have a business card to do business. Or is it?

THE CASE FOR A BUSINESS CARD

Getting a business card is an important step on your business journey. It signals you are in business—for real. When you meet someone, you now have something to give them that says *I'm in business; you can contact me.*

Even if you don't feel like you have everything figured out yet, make a card. You are sending out to the Universe *I am ready to be in business— here is my calling card.* And when someone asks, 'How can I contact you?' you will have a business card ready to give them.

> *I am in business—here is my card.*

In this chapter, I also make the case for doing without business cards. I want to be clear that I have business cards, but I'm committed to sustainability and prefer digital where possible. But I always have my cards with me so that when, say, a school mum suggests a play date, I have a card I can give her. You might be surprised how often that leads to that person becoming a listener of my podcast or buying my book or training course.

THE OLD-SCHOOL BUSINESS CARD

While many people have successfully ditched paper business cards, I believe they still play an important role. It's a bit like how people predicted we would have a paperless office; while a lot of things can now be done online—even signing and filing documents electronically—printers and copiers haven't become obsolete (yet).

Still, people who are passionate about sustainability (as I am) tend to be moving away from business cards. If you've ever stopped and pondered a large stack of business cards, many for people you can no longer remember, the thought that it's all a bit pointless might cross your mind.

Ah, but there is a point. While we are moving quickly towards digital options, at the time of writing, there is still an important societal role that business cards play. In certain cultures, notably in Asia, a business card is visually important. Presenting a business card is a ritual, an art form—as is receiving a business card. It reflects face and status.

While we are a bit more casual and egalitarian in Australia, being able to present a business card at functions still says something. I find it's often a great way to initiate a conversation, as in, 'Hi, my name is Serina and here's my business card. It's nice to meet you.' It's also handy to have a card on you when someone says, 'How can I contact you?' And it feels, well, professional.

For this reason, author Misty Henkel advises that it is essential to have business cards. She suggests people print in bulk and always have at least forty on them at any one time.

I am proud to share who I am and what my business does.

WHAT TO INCLUDE ON YOUR BUSINESS CARD

How elaborate do you need your business card to be? You don't need too much on your card, but you do need people to be able to contact you afterwards. You might think this would be obvious, but people often get it wrong.

According to Misty Henkel, a common problem is cards that don't include key contact information. 'Don't make it so hard for someone to contact you,' she says. 'Make it easy.' Complications can creep in when people want to direct you to funnels, or websites linked to social media handles or other things. 'If someone is already standing in front of you, you have gotten in contact with them,' she says. 'Make it easy for them to phone you or email you.'

Another common problem Misty sees is that people don't accurately describe what their business is. 'Sometimes you go to events and collect a lot of cards, then you come home, and you can't remember who gave you the card and it says nothing about what the business is really about,' she says. Again, this might seem obvious, but I've experienced this problem as well.

There are several essentials that a business card needs to include:

1. **Name.** This is not a legal document, so you want the name that you are commonly known by. If you were christened Catherine but are known as Cate, put Cate on your card.

2. **Business name.** If it's not clear what your business is from its name, then add a description. For instance, Jane & Smith Lawyers is clear, but Strategic Solutions is not. (I made this up, then googled and found there is a company with this name— they helpfully have a long 'What we do' section on their website.)

3. **What you do.** You might know what you do (most of the time, anyway). But do others? What is your core business? Are you a consultant? Writer? Cafe owner? In retail? Make it clear on your card.

4. **Logo or photo.** Your branding is important, so make sure you use this on your business card. It's not just about the graphic; ensure you follow through with the right colours and fonts. If you are in a service-based industry where you are your brand, a photo is a nice touch. For instance, if you are an MC, a marriage celebrant or even a real-estate agent, it can help to have your photo. It certainly makes it easier to remember you.

5. **Email.** People are increasingly on a range of social media platforms, but nothing beats an old-fashioned email. Make it easy for someone to email you.

6. **Phone number.** Just like including an email, you might think this is obvious, but it's not. Some people worry about their privacy. Honestly, if you are worried about your privacy, why are you in business or going to a networking event? Make it easy for people to find you.

7. **Social media details.** If you are on multiple platforms, it is tempting to list them all, but this makes your card look overwhelming. Consider instead something like, 'Find me on Facebook & Instagram'. If you are a prolific social media user, it might be enough to share your handle (e.g. @joyfulfrugalista).

There are also a few optional details you could include:

1. **QR code.** A QR code on a card can be a good way for people to connect with you. A younger, Asian demographic will appreciate a QR code. But do include more than just a code. Otherwise, your card will go into the 'I have no idea who gave me this card' pile.

2. **Double-sided printing.** It usually costs only a little extra to have the reverse side printed. The cost depends on the type of card and designer, but for a recent Vistaprint design, it worked out as an additional sixteen dollars for the reverse side of five hundred cards (three cents a card). You could use this to include extra

information, such as a QR code, an inspirational quote, or space for appointments. I have two of my businesses represented on the one card: *The Joyful Frugalista* on one side and *The Joyful Business Club* on the other.

3. **Thicker or nicer card, or embossed gloss.** You don't need to spend a lot of money on fancy card stock or having your cards embossed. It is, however, important that the cards feel sturdy rather than cheap. My cards for *The Joyful Fashionista* were accidentally printed on nicer card stock and they look and feel so lovely I will do this again in the future. It is, after all, about fashion.

4. **Non-standard size.** I like to make my business cards a standard size; there is nothing worse than not being able to fit business cards into a cardholder index. Some people might want to stand out by having big cards—or even wooden cards—but I generally feel the negatives outweigh the positives.

FRUGALISTA TIP

Proofread your business card carefully before you print it. Sound obvious? Little mistakes like a wrong digit in a phone number or a misspelt name are common and costly mistakes.

BUSINESS CARD ETIQUETTE

Never, ever write on a business card—unless the person who has given it to you suggests you add something to it. It is especially rude to write comments about the person on the card. I know it might aid your memory, but you're essentially saying, *I don't find you memorable enough.*

When you receive a business card, where possible, accept it with two hands. (If you are at a cocktail event, don't drop your drink on the floor just so that you can do this.) After receiving the card, take a moment to study it and make some polite remarks. It is a good opportunity for you to make a mental association so you can remember the person again.

According to Misty Henkel, the conventional advice is that you should wait for someone to hand you a business card and that you should never offer one first. She disagrees with this view, and I have flouted it for years and I will continue to do so. I'm the sort of person who likes to go up to people who look lonely at a networking event and introduce myself. Handing over my business card is a way to start a conversation or connection. I also find it easier to hand it over first, because you might want to migrate to another group after your chat, and sometimes it's easier to do that quietly (aka sneak off) rather than interrupt the flow of conversation.

THE CASE AGAINST THE BUSINESS CARD

At events at the Canberra Innovation Centre, I'm finding that more and more people are ditching business cards. Young people, in particular, are eschewing them for environmental reasons. It's not just because of the cardboard used in the printing; it's also the inks and the packaging. In these pandemic times, it's also good to avoid having more than one person touch things.

I'm working on a new networking group that plans to ban all business cards. Yep, a networking group with no business cards.

How do you give your contact details to others if you don't have a business card? There are several ways, including:

WECHAT

Do you use WeChat? If you are marketing to Chinese audiences, it's a good platform to be on. It's also one of the earliest platforms that encouraged the use of a QR code to make it easy for people to connect. While handing out business cards used to be an essential part of doing business in China, the WeChat revolution has changed everything. Whereas once business cards were a must-have in Chinese culture, now many people who want to connect say, 'Shall I scan you, or you scan me?'

I like to scan and connect on WeChat with Chinese Australians I meet at functions, and it is always a winner—one once reached out on WeChat afterwards and offered me a job! Devoted WeChat users love scanning each other's QR codes. And the key to networking is connecting with people on their preferred platform.

LINKEDIN

What does your LinkedIn account say about you? From going on a first date to considering a business deal, LinkedIn is the intel source of choice. Ensure your profile is up to date and reflects the business you wish to promote. For those side hustling as they transition out of work, this is not as easy as you might think; unlike Facebook, you can only have one profile rather than several.

One little-known feature of LinkedIn is that its mobile version includes a QR code. Simply scan someone's QR code and they will receive an invitation from you to connect. I learned this effective tip from Nick McNaughton. Nick refuses to accept business cards and, at the end of every training course he runs, encourages all participants to link up with each other via LinkedIn.

INSTAGRAM

Many business people, especially women, have Instagram accounts because it's a good (free) platform for building brand awareness—especially for products and services that are photogenic.

An easy way to connect at networking events is to get out your phone and look up someone else's Instagram account and follow it. It is one of the best gifts to give an emerging business. They will value your follow, and you can learn more about their brand.

But sometimes, it can be hard for people to get the right handle for your account—especially if you use unusual spelling. You can avoid problems with this by generating a QR code in Instagram (top-right hamburger menu > QR Code).

DESIGN YOUR OWN APP

Are you a tech aficionado? If so, you can always do what Rae Knopik did and design your own app. Rae, founder of the not-for-profit CBR Gals Network and startup GREN, has worked for tech startups and enjoyed the challenge of organising her app that allows people to scan in her contact details. 'It's always a talking point, and it was super easy to design,' she says.

CRM

Have you ever come away from a networking event with piles of cards? Months after receiving one, have you tried to find that card again? I can relate. When I worked in Taipei, I had hundreds of business cards in big fat piles. It could often be next to impossible to find important cards again without a method.

As a business owner, you must have a customer relationship management (CRM) system. It's especially important if you are going to a lot of networking events. Your system can be complex or easy depending on your time and budget. But you do need to at least have a system in place.

Here are a few ideas:

- **Business cardholders.** You can buy a business cardholder folder at any stationery store. You could have multiple cardholders for different themes. Or you can just put them all in one and at least they are together.

- **Index card systems.** Index card systems used to be popular in the pre-computer days, yet surprisingly, new ones are still being sold. I know this because I saw some at Officeworks recently. A business-card index system is great because it allows you to sort cards alphabetically and flick through until you find the ones you want.

- **Excel spreadsheet.** Before I had an online CRM tool, I used an Excel spreadsheet to track things like media and customer contacts. The advantage of a spreadsheet is that if you later upgrade to a professional CRM system, it will be easy to upload the data.

- **Free or simple CRM products.** You might not think you have any CRM products. But do you use Gmail? If so, do you use Google Contacts? Or what about the contact management system on your phone?

- **Bookkeeping software.** If you use online accounting software, it likely has a contacts database. While it is designed for recording details of vendors and customers, you could use it for more than just paying bills.

TIP

If you are not yet ready to invest in CRM software, start collating contacts and customers in an Excel spreadsheet or similar. Most CRM software systems make it easy to upload details from a spreadsheet, usually in CSV format. (It's easy to convert an Excel spreadsheet to CSV format.)

- **Dedicated CRM programs.** If you work in sales or plan to, investing in CRM software as your business expands can be a good move. I currently use the Zoho One suite of products, which enables me to sync all CRM data together in one place. The market leader is Salesforce, which is so popular it now has a market cap of USD226.19 billion. Salesforce has a variety of plans and is customisable, but like anything, it depends on your business needs.

EMAIL SIGNATURE BLOCK

Sometimes, people get so caught up with printing business cards and developing their social media channels that they overlook the obvious—their emails.

Do you have an email signature block? Most emails, including Gmail, can be easily customised to include a signature block. Develop one that has your key details, including your phone number, website, and social media handles. If someone needs to find you again, this makes it much easier for them to do so.

EXERCISES

1.

What does your business card say about you? How long has it been since you revamped yours? Or perhaps you don't you have one yet? Update your business card or design a new one.

2.

Do you have an email signature block? If not, set one up now. It's easier than you think. Observe some of the signature blocks of emails you receive. What did you like? What didn't you like?

3.

What CRM system do you have? If you don't have one, set up an Excel spreadsheet with contacts. If you do, is your CRM system sufficient for your needs? Do you know how it works? Are you using it to its full capacity?

7

MONEY

If you are running a business, money is going to be at the core of what you do. Even if you are so passionate about your 'why' that money isn't your motivation, you will need money coming in to have a sustainable business. When you are attracting sufficient money, it enables you to implement what you feel soul-called to do. And even if you are incorporated as a not-for-profit organisation, you won't be able to continue to exist if you can't show your supporters that you are good at managing money.

Yet there is so much reluctance to talk about money—something that I am passionate about overcoming in my work in *The Joyful Frugalista*. Bec Cuzzillo notes that money isn't something we need to be afraid of. 'The more we talk about it, the more it is normalised,' she says. 'You can earn money doing what you love. You can earn money doing something that fills your heart with purpose. You don't have to hustle hard. And you don't have to sell your soul.'

PREPARE A CASH BUFFER BEFORE YOU START

Some people are great at starting a business and earning money straight away, but most aren't. And it's unrealistic to put pressure on yourself to be earning money from the beginning if you don't have to. It's good to have the drive and ambition (you'll need it), but it's far better to save up before you start. Unexpected things can happen, and it's better to be prepared.

I had *almost* paid off the mortgage, hubby was in a stable job, I had good superannuation and four freelance writing clients when I decided to do the almost unthinkable and quit a stable and sought-after job in October 2019. I also had a stream of positively geared income from an Airbnb unit and hosted guests at home occasionally, and I had been sounded out about a more substantial opportunity.

Three weeks after leaving work, Canberra was immersed in strong smoke haze due to bushfires that lasted for almost three months. Airbnb bookings were cancelled. Then when the rains came, COVID arrived. This led to even more Airbnb cancellations, plus the disappearance of most paid freelance writing gigs.

It might sound terrible, and to be honest, there were times when I worried whether I had made the right decision. But it ended up being fine—more than fine. I pivoted to offering training courses and coaching, discovering that it was something I loved to do. Freelance writing opportunities returned, and my podcast took off. I'm not saying it was easy, but because I had a financial buffer, I felt more confident about trying new things and pivoting. It also meant I panicked less.

Two years on and we have paid off the mortgage, have a growing share portfolio and a higher overall net worth due to property investments that have gone up in the boom. Who would have thought? I've also started new ventures and received grant funding to help get them off the ground. I credit all of this to being in a good financial situation to start with.

I embrace abundance.

CASHFLOW

Sadly, one of the biggest reasons businesses fail is due to cashflow issues. Cashflow broadly means that you have enough money coming in to meet your expenses. Sometimes, even profitable businesses can fail due to cashflow problems, caused by not being paid by those who owe them money, disruptive events such as COVID, spending or losing money set aside for expenses, not setting aside money for expenses, theft or fraud.

As outlined in Chapter 9, there are many systems available now that allow small businesses to do their bookkeeping online. Whether you use a spreadsheet for a side hustle starting out, hire a bookkeeper, or have a chief financial officer, you need to be across your money. You need to be comfortable with monitoring what is happening with your business and its cashflow. Even if you have outsourced to someone else, you still need to look at the data carefully and regularly ask questions.

Thankfully, it is not hard for most startups to know what is happening with their cashflow. Most online systems will have a function allowing you to monitor cashflow: e.g. a profit and loss summary. This will allow you to see at a glance whether or not you are actually making money from your business, or whether you are going backwards. It will also highlight unpaid invoices.

If you don't have an online accounting system, even just looking at your bank statements—regularly—is a good place to start. It is important to make sure you know where your money is going.

This might sound obvious, but the obvious isn't always easy.

In a podcast interview on *The Joyful Frugalista,* Amy Bett shared how she left a corporate role to start an events management business. She thought she was doing well as she had lots of clients and was super busy. What she didn't fully understand was the true cost of hosting the events, and when all costs were factored in, the business was going backwards. It's an easy mistake to make: you quote low or offer items cheaply, wanting to attract customers. Or you seek business not knowing the true costs of your product, aka your break-even price. If you go too low, you won't be able to build a sustainable business. And if everyone wants you, it's likely a sign that you aren't charging enough.

Cashflow cycles also affect businesses even if they are profitable. For instance, a business owner recently told me how he landed a lucrative long-term contract with a government client. The issue is his business is now moving away from a cashflow model of many small jobs that pay regularly to incorporate a larger client that pays much less regularly.

In my business, I used to invoice my main freelance writing client each month. They would then pay two to four weeks later. This meant that it could be six to eight weeks before I was paid, and that I received funds in my bank account much less predictably than when I was drawing a public service salary.

And of course, you might have to chase unpaid invoices. Sometimes someone just forgets or thought they had paid but hadn't (I've been guilty of forgetting to hit the final approval button when making payments online). Or maybe the invoice gets lost in the mail or goes to their spam box in email—again, it does happen. Or maybe the client's policy is not to pay unless chased. I once knew a lady who worked for a company whose policy was never to pay unless they received a call asking for payment of unpaid money. I think that's a disreputable way to run a business, but some people do it.

Also ensure that you keep good records, including receipts. A successful business (legally) claims all the business expenses it is entitled to on tax and has records to prove it. The successful business doesn't fear an ATO audit, because its financial affairs are in good order, with receipts and evidence of allowable deductions on file. I scan in my invoices and add them to my online accounting system (Zoho Books) so that everything is neat and together.

FRUGAL TIP

The Australian Taxation Office allows claims for self-education and study expenses where it relates to current employment activities. Keep your receipt—you might be able to claim the cost of this book when doing your tax.

For information on eligibility to claim self-education expenses, see the ATO website.[21]

I operate with financial integrity and I attract customers who also act with integrity with their money.

GRANT MONEY

Want to get a new idea off the ground or build your existing business? One way to turbocharge what you are doing is through grant funds.

In 2021, I was blessed to receive two sets of grant funding to build *The Joyful Fashionista*. Yep, not one, but two. The funding was significant for me, not just because of the cash injection, but also because I felt it confirmed that I was on the right track. Being awarded that grant funding gave me a tremendous confidence boost. It also led to some high-profile media and lent my startup credibility.

CASE STUDY
Synthesis Organics

Theme Rains served as Australia's national ambassador for Women's Entrepreneurship Day from 2019 to 2021. Her business, Synthesis Organics, manufactures essential oils and organic products in the Northern Rivers region of New South Wales.

In September 2021, Synthesis Organics was awarded $460,000 in grant funding from the New South Wales Government as part of the Regional Job Creation Fund. The company will use the funding to establish a new company headquarters that will include a start-of-the-art lab and facilities for the extraction and manufacture of essential oils, distribution, training, administration, and workshops. In all, around twenty-three new jobs will be created as a result of the grant funding.

Think you could never get any grant funding? The first thing to do is find eligible grants. Where possible, go to information sessions to understand the organisation and what the grant funding is for. And of course, spend time on the application.

Some good sources for finding grant funding are:

- **GrantConnect.** This is an Australian Government site that brings together all grant funding rounds across government into one place.

- **State/territory resources.** Most states and territories will fund grants for social, community, environmental, and local business initiatives. You might be surprised what is on offer, especially initiatives designed to rebuild after COVID, bushfires, floods or other disasters, or to promote certain priorities, such as regional development.

- **Local Government resources.** You might not think that your local government has any grant funding or other initiatives, but you might be surprised. There are often initiatives funded to help the local community. There are also sometimes opportunities aligned with sister-city relationships overseas (in non-COVID times).

- **Your local politician.** Your elected representative is likely to want to share good news about grant funding opportunities, especially for community initiatives or those aimed at creating jobs. Read newsletters or other materials, search websites or consider (if it aligns with your political views) to follow on social media.

- **Boosting Female Founders Initiative.** Recognising the comparative difficulties that female founders face in obtaining start-up funds, the Boosting Female Founders Initiative is an Australian Government grant program that provides competitive grant funding to female founders.

- **Innovation hubs/networks.** Being connected will help you learn more about grant rounds that may be coming up. Some innovation hubs may have grant funding, but the advantage of being connected is that you can be part of the chatter about opportunities coming up.

- **Expert FindHer.** The Expert FindHer website is a (relatively) recent database established by CSIRO and the Department of Industry, Science, Energy and Resources. The website complements the Boosting Female Founders Initiative by providing information on support for female founders, including grant funding opportunities.

- **Banks and credit unions.** Many financial institutions have corporate social responsibility programs that include funding for female entrepreneurs, including social enterprises. These are often focused on building stronger communities, but sometimes eligibility is broader than just not for profits.

The second thing you need to do is craft a good application. I used to manage the Australia-China Secretariat, an organisation that had an annual grant funding round. I was the first person to read, shortlist and comment on applications before consultation with other divisions and departments. I was also responsible for compiling the lists that went to the board for decision. I've also been on the other side, applying for grants. Here are some of my top tips for writing a winning application:

1. **Ensure you meet the eligibility requirements.** Often, people spend a lot of time drafting an application, only to realise they aren't eligible to apply. I'm often looking at grants for my Zonta club, and they generally require things like registration with the Australian Charities and Not-for-profits Commission. Other grants may require Australian or other citizenship, residency in a city or regional area, a particular gender or ethnicity, or registration as a student or graduate.

2. **Read the selection criteria.** If the grant has guidelines or selection criteria, make sure you understand them and respond. Applications are often ranked by criteria, so you need to address each part. In the case of my previous role, we had an online form where assessors could rank by criteria and give a final score. This then aided the board in making a shortlist.

3. **Never copy and paste.** Someone reading a copy-and-pasted

application can generally tell that little thought has gone into it. A common (and unsuccessful) grant application that I have come across is a recycled pitch for academic funding. Not only do these recycled applications not meet the selection criteria, but the terminology is completely different (think terms like 'methodology', 'field research' and 'academic conference' rather than explaining how the grant will meet the purpose).

4. **Have a clear project and funding request.** Having been both an unsuccessful and successful grant applicant, I believe that what got me across the line with *The Joyful Fashionista* was that I was clear about what the project was and how the funds would be used. It also helps if you have a clear metric that can be used to show how you will have successfully used the funds and how that aligns with the grant purposes: e.g. deliver training for fifty students, build a website, write a report, create ten new jobs. Having a project that is clear—and interesting—also helps with media.

The third thing to consider is what to do if you are successful in obtaining a grant. In many ways, this is just the beginning.

1. **Understand your grant agreement.** You will generally be required to sign a formal contract known as a grant agreement. Before signing, you need to be clear about your obligations and raise any concerns you might have about things like participating in the media, intellectual property ownership, and your obligations for things like child protection policies and obeying the law.

2. **Understand how grant funds can be spent.** Grant funding will usually have rules about what it can and can't be used for. Generally, if you have received funding for a particular purpose, you can only spend it on that. For instance, if my Zonta club received funding to help domestic violence survivors with home-starter packs, it would not be appropriate to use those funds for scholarships for women in STEM (science, technology,

engineering and maths). In this scenario, even if they ended up with more funds than they needed for the packs, they would probably need to go back to the organisation providing the grant and discuss it. This may result in a variation to the grant agreement or, more likely, a return of unspent funds.

3. **Grant funding is rarely for your salary.** You might think that as a startup you have struck gold when you receive grant funding. Finally, you can splurge a bit because you're in the money. Unfortunately, grant funding is rarely for existing work, including your salary. It is usually to fund new initiatives (or provide matched funding where you can contribute money or time).

4. **You will need to acquit the grant.** At the end of the period specified in the grant agreement, you will need to acquit your grant. This means that you will need to account for how you have spent the money. Ensuring you have receipts and time logs is important, but it's even more important to demonstrate how your project achieved the goals of the grant program. You might think this is unnecessary paperwork, but in my experience as a grant manager, this is vitally important. Often, an organisation cannot fund you again if you haven't acquitted funds—even if they know it's been a good project. Keep in mind that the grant organisation needs to demonstrate that it has properly managed its grant funding, especially if it is a government organisation or has a board.

5. **Communicate.** Don't just take the money and run—ensure you communicate progress with the grant organisation. A good way to do this is to send them semi-regular emails (or newsletters) about progress. Most grant organisations will ask you to acknowledge their contribution online and on social media. Make sure you understand their brand guidelines and use their logo and other assets appropriately.

GOVERNMENT AND OTHER INCENTIVES

Beyond grant funding, the Federal Government, state and territory governments and sometimes even local governments have financial incentives aimed at stimulating local business. A tax accountant is generally well versed in available programs and can advise on eligibility.

At the time of writing, these are a few programs you might want to investigate:

- **COVID hardship incentives.** If you are a business that has suffered a drop in revenue due to COVID, you may be eligible for support payments or even a grant. For instance, the New South Wales Government offers JobSaver payments and microgrants. The policy is constantly changing, so it is important to check government websites. Above all, don't just assume it doesn't apply to you—you don't know unless you investigate and apply.

  treasury.gov.au/coronavirus

- **Accelerating Commercialisation program.** This is designed for Australian entrepreneurs, researchers, inventors and startups who have a novel product, process or service they want to commercialise. Successful recipients can receive expert advice and guidance, and up to $1 million of matched project funding.

- **CSIRO Kick-Start.** Companies that are less than three years old and have an annual turnover of less than $1.5 million can apply to partner with CSIRO and receive up to $50,000 in matched funding. The program is aimed at supporting Australian innovation by supporting companies in the research and testing stage, and the grant is designed for companies researching a new idea, or testing or developing a novel product or service.

- **Research and Development Tax Incentive.** The Australian Government provides a tax offset to encourage innovation. Since 1 July 2016, companies with an annual turnover below $20 million have been able to claim a 43.5% refundable tax offset against research and development expenditure. An accountant can provide advice on eligibility.

GETTING INVESTORS

For most startups, the pathway is to develop an idea and pitch it to investors. And according to Nick McNaughton, there has never been a better time for entrepreneurs to seek investor funding. Nick knows this from experience; as CEO of ANU Connect Ventures and founder of Campus Plus, he regularly makes successful pitches to investors. He also invests in startups—both as an angel investor and providing venture capital. He delivers a popular course about how startups can find grant funding or get investors at the Canberra Innovation Network.

There are several avenues you might consider when seeking an investor, including:

- **Angel groups.** Many capital cities have angel groups (e.g. Sydney Angels, Capital Angels). And there is even an angel investor group that invests in female founders—Scale Investors. An angel investor is someone who provides capital for a business or startup. An angel investor can sometimes support a new idea or business earlier than when most investors can back them. An angel will want a return on their investment usually by way of convertible debt or ownership equity. But more than the money, angels are often experienced businesspeople who want to offer support and guidance.

- **Venture capital firms.** Venture capital financing is a form of equity financing where a firm provides funding in exchange for part ownership. Venture capitalists are usually able to provide greater funding than angel investors and will usually want a larger equity stake. As of the time of writing, there are around 120 venture-capital firms that have invested in Australian startups.[22] Some of the best known in Australia are Blackbird Ventures, Brandon Capital, Telstra Ventures and Square Peg Capital.

- **Startup incubator and accelerator programs.** Many innovation centres have accelerator programs where you will be matched with a mentor who is often also an investor. Sometimes, the programs themselves provide grant funding (e.g. as a COVID rebuilding measure), or they offer an opportunity to pitch to investors during the program. Inclusion in the programs is generally competitive. Programs include SproutX, Startmate, the Founders Program (UNSW Sydney), GRIFFIN Accelerator (Canberra Innovation Network) and BlueChilli (Sydney based).

- **LinkedIn.** LinkedIn isn't just for finding a job; you can also use it strategically to find potential investors. Don't sound like you are a scammer offering an 'investment opportunity', but instead, use it to build strategic relationships with leaders in your field.

An advantage of investor funding is that it will allow your startup to scale. It is useful if you are looking to grow quickly. An added advantage is that the investment often comes with access to experienced business professionals who can help and guide you.

A disadvantage of this type of funding is that you generally need to give up a share of ownership. You might not want your investor to take an active leadership role. As one female founder told me, 'I left my job because I felt I was being discriminated against as a woman. The last thing I want is to have a male investor tell me how to run my business. I prefer to bootstrap rather than seek an investor.'

Another key disadvantage is that globally, women are much less likely to receive start-up funding than men. In 2020, only 2.4% of female-led startups received funding (and the number declines to 0.2% when we talk about women of colour). There are several reasons for this. For one thing, investors are more likely to be men, and they are more likely to be looking for opportunities in sectors that are traditionally male-dominated, such as big tech. And men who pitch are more likely to razzle-dazzle during a short, high-octane pitch than women.

CASE STUDY
Pinky Gloves

In April 2021, Eugen Raimkulow and Andre Ritterswürden pitched a product on Die Höhle der Löwen (The Lions' Cave), a Shark Tank-style program. One of the male judges liked the pitch and invested EUR30,000. The product? Pink disposable gloves that could be used for removing and disposing of tampons. The plastic gloves would prevent women from getting blood on their hands and allow the tampons to be wrapped in plastic for disposal. The problem? Apart from the plastic gloves creating additional waste, it contributed to stigmatising menstruation.[23]

In their pitch, the inventors said they came up with the idea after living with female housemates. They felt that there wasn't a sanitary way to dispose of tampons, and said they would see red blood on toilet paper covering the tampons in the bin, and that 'after a while, it just smells unpleasant.'[24]

After the episode aired, there was widespread outcry from many women and women's rights organisations. The investor later apologised. Raimkulow and Ritterswürden said they had been subjected to hate speech.

But as Angela Priestley pointed out in an article on Women's Agenda, this case highlights how men received funding to solve a 'problem' they had no personal experience of while female startups continue to struggle to get funding. For instance, the investors on the same television show did not award any investment to German startup Ooia, which sells period underwear and nursing bras.[25]

CROWDSOURCING

An increasingly popular way to attract money for a startup or project is to crowdsource funding. There are now many platforms, including Kickstarter (often used for innovative startups) and GoFundMe (often used for charitable purposes).

An advantage of the crowdfunding mechanism is it allows you to test the market before you begin production. Rather than, for instance, spending money writing and publishing a book, you can crowdsource to raise funds—and validate proof of concept in the process.

There are, broadly, four types of crowdfunding:[26]

1. **Donation based.** This is typically a donation to support a cause, such as helping people out through personal crises (e.g. cancer treatment, bushfire recovery), or for a charitable cause (building or repairing a church). As a donor, you don't expect anything in return except for warm fuzzies. This model could be useful for community-based innovations.

2. **Debt based.** Debt-based funding is useful for businesses with a steady cashflow, who want a loan of money and undertake to service the loan with interest. It's essentially a form of peer-to-peer lending, and can be useful for when a business needs funds to scale up or start out (e.g. buy new stock, purchase a new computer, secure the lease of new premises). I founded *The Joyful Business Club* with the (long term) aim of providing a form of peer-to-peer lending for female startups.

3. **Equity based.** This model involves individuals giving shares in their business in exchange for capital investment. This model, known as equity crowdfunding, is becoming increasingly popular with startups and involves them raising money from a large number of investors.[27] Examples include Lift Women, Cake Equity, Equitise and VentureCrowd.

4. **Reward based.** This model involves raising money in return

for a product or service. For example, I gave money to a local author for a book on local Canberra stories. When he wrote the book and had it published, he provided me with a copy.

CASE STUDY
Community Toolbox Canberra

A group of Canberrans passionate about sustainability decided to create a tool library. The idea was that people could save money and be more sustainable by sharing resources.

The group started a crowdfunding campaign on the platform StartSomeGood with the aim of raising at least $7,000, which was the tipping point needed to make their project viable. They also nominated a stretch goal of $12,000. To encourage people to donate, they suggested contributions such as a $55 package for access to tools for a year; a $150 Father's Day gift that included aprons and an invitation to the launch; right up to $1,500, a lifetime membership that provided merch, other benefits and even a song written in their donor's honour.

The campaign was released on 14 July 2021. Within twelve hours, it attracted thirty-four per cent of its goal. It reached its $7,000 tipping point within a week and attracted $16,447 in funding. After a lockdown due to COVID that put all activities on hold for several months, it opened to the public on 6 November 2021.

> I'm a founding member and have enjoyed borrowing baking equipment from Community Toolbox Canberra. They have some great kitchen tools, including a waffle iron, ice-cream maker and baking tins.

My community supports me. All I have to do is ask.

LOANS

Once upon a time, getting a bank loan was the main way businesses sought to get more money as they expanded. The problem was that bank loans were hard to get—especially for women—and were generally only available to conventional businesses. Some loans also required home residences to be used as equity, or a family member to agree to be a guarantor.

While banks don't give money for nothing and need to be satisfied with the fundamentals of a business (make sure you have your business plan ready), I anticipate that (especially in a climate of low interest rates) bank lending will become more streamlined. Currently, banks will usually have a business lending area with loan officers who are experts at working with businesses and assessing risk. There are even new entrants such as Judo Bank, whose mandate is to work solely with small and medium enterprises.

Beyond banks, there are many avenues to get a loan. For instance, startups in the ACT can apply for funding from Epicorp, which provides lending and venture debt to emerging startups.

A key advantage in taking out a loan rather than seeking investors is that you retain ownership. Investors will often require an equity stake in a business, or at the very least will want to make their opinions about how you run your business known. While a bank will likely require security for its loan (e.g. a mortgage), so long as you repay, it is not likely to interfere in the day-to-day management of your business.

A disadvantage of a loan is that you are usually locked into making repayments at fixed times (e.g. mortgages are usually monthly). Businesses rarely have the same level of regular cashflow as someone drawing a wage, and you need to be prepared to repay in bad times as well as good. If your business is a cafe in a beach town that is quiet outside of school holidays, you will still need to be making repayments even when you aren't selling much coffee to tourists.

SALES

Sometimes, incubation programs and the chatter around startups direct founders towards equity funding. But there's another way to raise money: from sales of your product or services.

Sales are important as it's not just about money in the bank, but proof of concept. People might say they like something if you ask them to fill out a survey, but will they buy it? Selling products and services and having that as a key metric tells you about whether you have what the market wants. And even if you do go down the investor or loan route, being able to show good income from sales will help.

If you are uncomfortable selling, you need to get over it. Successful businesses are good at sales. That might sound harsh, but selling often involves putting yourself out there and doing things that make you feel uncomfortable—like pitching to people you don't know. You can hire salespeople and marketing professionals, but often, selling comes down to you. You are your company's best asset when it comes to sales, as you are what people see when they see your company.

People often buy from people. Why are Apple products so successful? You could say it is because of its innovation, but not everyone who works in tech would agree. Certainly, they are not the best value for money and some other products have the same or better functionality. Largely, the success of Apple is due to the charisma of founder Steve Jobs, who created an almost cult-like following. Whether you are an Apple user or not, you will have a view about Apple products. And I've learnt that it's best not to get into an argument with Apple aficionados: they love Apple products and will defend them no matter what.

> *I am proud to sell my products and services.*

Selling is a learnt skill. Salespeople aren't always pushy and aggressive. The successful ones rarely are. What they are is persistent and courageous, and experts in listening, solving problems, and they believe (or at least understand) what they are selling. Good communication often involves listening and building long-term relationships, rather than forcing someone to buy a product or service.

When selling your product or services, you also want to make it super easy for people. Don't make people jump through complicated funnels or processes. One of Amazon's successes is its invention of the one-click sales process—once set up, it's super easy. Make sure your product is easy to find on your website or socials, that payment processes work, and that you have a physical product on you at all times to sell.

For example, if you are going to a networking function, take a few copies of your book or product with you. If someone wants to buy it from you, you could give them your PayID so they can pay directly into your account, or you could even have a Square Reader so they can swipe their card straight away.

> *It's easy to buy from me.*

GET A 'REAL' JOB

When I left my full-time job in 2019 to pursue my entrepreneurial dreams, I thought I had quit for good. Yet in 2021, I found myself back in the same department, doing similar work to when I left eighteen months before.

Why would I do that? Well, for one thing, I was approached. I felt flattered, but I also felt that it was a good thing to reconnect and re-establish my credentials. It was part of Plan B just in case my main plans didn't work.

But being approached also coincided with deciding to commit funds to develop and market *The Joyful Fashionista*. We had funds from the sale of an investment property and grant funding, but I felt that going back to work and earning funds offered me a degree of stability and countered the fear of failure. As it turned out, doing something where I had expertise helped boost my confidence—especially when dealing with the uncertainties of a new venture.

Often, a new business or startup will take longer or cost more to get off the ground than we think. Or it may encounter difficulties (think COVID). Even if you have saved up beforehand, and even if initial sales are going well, you might need more cash.

I'm open to receiving abundance in expected and unexpected forms.

What can happen is that concerns about money and cashflow can lead us down a path of anxiety and worry, triggering a scarcity mindset. It's hard to be chipper and positive about your multi-million-dollar startup potential when you are struggling to pay for school uniforms, rent, and groceries.

CASE STUDY
Rachel Service

Rachel Service, CEO of Happiness Concierge and author of There Has to Be More, was facing burnout in her career. After bursting into tears on the subway after a Beyoncé concert, she realised she needed to make big life changes—including quitting her job. She is now a successful business owner but admits to having regularly woken up at 4:00 am in the early days, worrying about how she would pay bills. She took up a part-time job working in a cafe on weekends to balance her business as it grew. 'I felt I needed to balance the risk of starting a business with the security of cashflow, especially as I hired more people,' she says. 'But I didn't want something that would take up a cognitive load.'

Rachel also maintained good professional contacts and continues to put funds aside for a rainy day. 'You never know when you will need that money or have a surprising tax bill,' she says.

NOT-FOR-PROFITS AND SOCIAL ENTERPRISES

It's not wrong to earn money from our business. Having a business that produces an abundant income allows us to continue doing what we do. Not everyone is (like me) inherently frugal and close to financial independence. We need to find the money for food, accommodation, holidays, healthcare, family needs, etc., etc., etc.

I had a great podcast chat on *The Joyful Frugalista* with OzHarvest founder Ronni Kahn AO. She shared that she had been asked to speak at a school about finding purpose. She didn't tell the students that working for money was bad. Rather, she encouraged them to earn money, because that meant they had the means to share some of their wealth with others.

But having profit as the only motive for your business idea can lead you to doing what you don't love. Profit at any cost unrelated to values can lead to corrupt behaviours and produce environmentally unsustainable industries.

Many people choose to do what they do to make a difference rather than earn a big income. And that's okay. More than okay. It's not a contest to see who earns the most billions—it's what you are contributing back to society that will bring you happiness. Some people might choose to start a not-for-profit to fulfil their 'why', or join an existing one. And sometimes, doing something that is authentic and values-based might just make you wealthy.

CASE STUDY
The CBR Gals Network

Rae Knopik founded the CBR Gals Network after moving to Canberra. Rae, who is originally from Florida, met her partner in Florence, Italy, and, after following him back to Canberra, realised she didn't know a lot of people. She started an Instagram page, which gained traction and morphed into a network connecting women in the Canberra region. The CBR Gals Network now holds events and other activities to connect and inspire Canberra women.

The CBR Gals Network is incorporated as a not-for-profit (NFP). Rae decided to structure the organisation this way as she felt the community would understand and trust an NFP more readily than a social enterprise or other models. While the Network makes money from events and activities, the funds need to go back into the organisation. While Rae is the founder, the Network has a board and staff that oversee and implement activities.

NFP and social enterprise are terms that are often used interchangeably, but they are not the same. Social enterprises are a relatively new class of business, but they are growing. Unlike NFP organisations, they are allowed to make a profit. But the organisation undertakes to give some, or all, of their profits to purposes that do good in the world. The purpose of the business usually is aimed at helping the community or another cause in some way. A social enterprise can fundraise, but it does not enjoy the same tax concessions as an NFP.

CASE STUDY
The Mill House Ventures

Many people want to start businesses with the aim of doing social good. Recognising this, The Mill House Ventures is designed to help people establish and thrive in their social enterprise.

The Mill House Ventures is founded by Cindy Mitchell, a passionate advocate for civil society and social enterprise and social-impact investment movements globally. Cindy has worked as a venture capital investment manager and in corporate roles in the US and Australia—as well as executive roles in the Australian public service. She is also founder and CEO of No Sweat Fashions, a not-for-profit social enterprise aimed at providing employment and work experience for migrants and refugees, and was recognised as ACT Woman of the Year in 2020.

The Mill House Ventures runs a Social Enterprise Accelerator course that provides skills and networks to enable social enterprises to become sustainable. (And yes, The Mill House Ventures believes that you CAN accelerate a social enterprise.) It also runs a clinic that assists social and Indigenous ventures by connecting them with professional services, with the aim of assisting them to connect with the right services at the right time.

EXERCISES

1.

How do you feel about money? How comfortable are you being paid for what you offer? Write down your feelings around money.

2.

How does your business track its cashflow? What could be improved? Commit to finding some time each week to look at the cashflow of your business.

3.

Investigate avenues for grant funding and write a list of the grants you could apply for. Consider going to an information session or speaking to someone who has successfully received grant funding.

4.

Who is your ideal investor? Write a few words about what they would look like, their background and their interests, and the value the investment would bring to your business.

5.

How could you improve sales for your business? What could you do to make it easier for people to buy from you?

6.

What is the financial goal of your business? Is it to be a social enterprise, to be a small-scale solopreneur, or to scale up into a multi-billion-dollar company?

8

BUILDING
YOUR TEAM

You've got a great idea, and you are excited to start. Who better to develop it with than your BFF (best friend forever)? Or maybe someone who has technical skills, such as computer coding, that you don't have?

When people start a business for the first time, their inclination is often to go into partnership with friends or family. Sometimes, it can work out fabulously well. Other times, it can be a disaster.

But whether you go solo or have partners, one thing is for certain: you need to build strong teams. Just like raising a child, your business needs a village for it to succeed.

GOING INTO PARTNERSHIP WITH A FRIEND OR FAMILY MEMBER

Going into partnership with someone you know and like can be lots of fun—at least, at first. It makes sense in terms of how the ideas often happen. Say you are having coffee, one of you comes up with a crazy idea, and the other person goes, 'Yeah, I totally get that, and ...' Within minutes, you have sketched out some ideas on a paper napkin (or written some things on your phone) and your business partnership is born.

A good friend can know you better than you know yourself, and working with them can seem like an obvious next step. But friendship and a business relationship are not always the same.

The last time I saw my grandfather, when he was in hospital shortly before he died, he gave me some advice. 'Never go into business with family or friends,' he said. 'If you're going to go into business, do it yourself.'

I will never know why he decided to tell me that. At that point, I was at university studying law—and Chinese. Starting a business was not on my radar. I've never forgotten his words, but I've frequently acted against his advice.

I've tried twice to form partnerships: once with my podcast co-host and a second time in the early days of what became *The Joyful Business Club*. Both times, it was with someone I really liked and got along with. I loved the buzz of positive energy and the ability to bounce around ideas; the synergy that came with sharing. And to be honest, I was hoping that the business relationship would cement a growing friendship. I craved that close connection. But both times, the relationship crashed and burned—badly.

You would think I have learnt my lesson, but I haven't. I still value collaboration, and it hasn't stopped me from looking for business partners.

When I was developing *The Joyful Fashionista*, I wanted to bring a partner on board. I had two people in mind; one even came to meetings regularly but was unable to become a formal partner due to a conflict-of-interest issue. I will be forever grateful to her for her help, encouragement and insights, and hope that in the karma of life, I can repay her. The second person just wasn't interested. I appreciated her forthrightness and honesty.

The key problem with forming a partnership with a friend (or family member) is that it's easy for things to spill over to the personal. I'm sad to have lost two people I considered friends. Both times, the fallout was emotionally hard to deal with. And I discovered that just because you are friends with someone, doesn't mean you are going to work together well as business partners. Are you going to be able to share a similar commitment to the business as it grows?

It happens all the time. Microsoft was originally founded by Paul Allen, who convinced his mate Bill Gates to quit Harvard and join him. Gates became more committed (obsessed?) with work, coding through the night, while Allen wanted to do other things like play guitar and watch space shuttle launches. Allen left in 1983 after he was diagnosed with Hodgkin's disease (an aggressive type of cancer). Who can blame someone confronted with the possibility of imminent mortality to want to work less and seek greater meaning in life? And as this story showed, while two people may have been close friends at high school, they may still grow apart professionally. Both developed different goals and visions as they grew up.

Despite everything, I have partner envy. I crave having a close partnership with a gal pal. I see other people who have amazing relationships with a business partner and I can imagine them bouncing around ideas together on their way to creating a joint empire. I so want that relationship.

Yet what appears on the outside to be a great partnership might not be a true reflection of what is going on. You rarely know someone fully until there is a dispute, problem or disagreement. That's when someone's true nature comes out: their resilience, commitment, and ability to take ownership of issues rather than play the blame game.

International award-winning psychic medium and published author Suzy Cherub voiced to me that many of her clients ask for intuitive and practical advice about resolving partnership challenges. They might not admit to these difficulties in public, but partnership complications are real and can cause trepidation. Regardless, Suzy is still optimistic about co-creative collaborations, as she continues to have many fruitful working relationships, including a successful one with her daughter, Bec Cuzzillo, with the two regularly co-hosting training sessions.

CASE STUDY
Mums in Business Association

Estelle Keeber and Leona Burton are stepsisters who, according to media reports, had always been close. Both were battlers who had done it tough. Estelle was a single mother who had once relied on a food bank to feed her family. To overcome mental health issues, she started taking photography courses at night and went on to build a successful photography business. Burton was a mother of five who had experience in starting up several businesses. Both identified a need to make networking more accessible to mothers with young children; the traditional business breakfast model didn't work for mums busy getting kids to school.

Estelle and Leona started Mums in Business Association, an organisation that facilitated in-person networking for mums and women around the world. They authored and edited several bestselling books, including their autobiography Laid Bare, ran courses, were featured in publications such as Forbes, and became social media stars. Their business turned over more than GBP1 million a year annually and it looked like nothing could stop them.

I was super excited to find out more about this successful power-sister duo. I summoned a bit of courage and asked Estelle to be a guest on The Joyful Frugalista podcast. To my delight, she said yes. We recorded a Zoom interview late one evening in May (early morning in the UK). I was inspired and motivated by her energy and came away feeling like anything was possible. Boom! I wanted their secret for success. It seemed like they had the perfect partnership, with Estelle telling me in glowing terms how Leona was the one who had the big vision that inspired Mums in Business Association.

The next day, I woke up to the news that Leona had put out a tearful tell-all Facebook Live announcing that the sisters had split. According to Leona, underlying problems had come to the fore over a leadership tussle and she had been pushed out. Amid personal attacks from members of the community, Estelle went silent. Leona has now created Mums in Business International, and Estelle has a social-media training business called Immortal Monkey.

Former Mums in Business Association groups in Australia have disbanded and several new splinter groups have formed in their place.

As discussed in Chapter 2, it's important to be aware that with a partnership, unlike with a company structure, all partners are jointly and severally liable for the partnership. So if you have a partner who gets into massive debt on behalf of the company, you will have to pay— even if you didn't know about it.[28] This is why it is important to have a partnership agreement in place.

GETTING OUT OF A PARTNERSHIP

Anton Pemmer has seen and experienced it all when it comes to partnerships. Anton is the owner of INVO8YOU and is contracted as a business advisor at the Southern Region Business Enterprise Centre, and also lectures on Innovation and Entrepreneurship to postgrads and MBA students at the Australian National University. He's been in business with partners. 'I've dealt with fraud with a partner, and partners who seem to create problems when wanting to separate and to this day, I don't know why,' he says.

Anton says often a partnership will go well until something unforeseen happens, such as a health issue affecting a family member, or a major life event. I would add that with women in business, it could be falling pregnant or taking on other caring roles (such as caring for an elderly parent). At this point, the partner needs to know how they can exit, or as Anton says, 'What is my get-out-of-jail card?

'The biggest issue with any partnership is that no one has discussions about how to get out,' Anton says. 'It's important to have very transparent discussions at the beginning, especially about how you calculate the value of your business and the stake of each partner.'

Anton suggests that partners and co-founders use a tool to measure contribution, such as Slicing Pie.[29] This software allows business owners to amortise the difference between contributions. For instance, one partner has money but doesn't have time. Meanwhile, one is providing sweat equity working on the business and thinks the other partner isn't doing anything. Slicing Pie enables both partners to record their respective contributions to gain greater visibility.

Anton also suggests it is important to record sweat-equity contributions based on market value. 'Often we do costings based on ourselves but we should be doing costings based on hiring a staff member ... This is important as we scale,' he says.

Having been down the road of experiencing a partnership implode—twice—I believe some of the problems could have been averted if we had had some honest conversations at the beginning. It's easier to do this when there is positive momentum and things are going well. But both times, I had been more focused on getting things up and running: deciding on a name, designing a logo, applying for grants and doing a website. As the relationship seemed to be going well, I didn't take the time to query underlying assumptions.

QUESTIONS TO ASK A BUSINESS PARTNER

- What are the key strengths and skills you would bring to the partnership?
- How much time are you willing to invest?
- How will we make decisions?
- Who makes the decisions?
- How much money are you willing to put in?
- Who will stump up the initial costs? How will this person be reimbursed?
- Who will own the assets of the business, including domain names and equipment?
- What is your endgame? Would you consider selling?
- What is your preferred mechanism of communication? (e.g. scheduled meetings, frequent Facebook messenger chats when ideas strike, emails, phone)
- How often do you want to communicate? And do you need time-out times or are you happy to have constant chatter?
- How do you handle stress and upset? How do you want your partner to support you through it?
- What are your values?
- What is your vision of the company's growth? Would you like it to remain small or scale up?
- What role do you see yourself playing in the company?
- What do you want to get out of the experience of being in business? (e.g. money, flexibility)
- Would you consider bringing on another partner or co-founder?
- What level of delegation, responsibility or consensus is required for the domains of the business?
- What is your risk appetite?
  - ☐ What does low risk and high risk look like to you?
- How serious are you about making the business work?

- How much time are you willing to invest before seeing success?
  - ☐ What does early success look like?
- How do we put a monetary value on each partner's contribution?

As I was exiting my second non-performing partnership, my husband asked me an insightful question: 'Why did you seek out this partnership in the first place?' When I stopped to think about it, I was choosing to go into partnerships with others because I thought I wasn't good enough. 'You are more than good enough,' he said.

As we will see in the next section, there are times when it is a good idea to bring on board partners who have the skills you need to build your business and take it forward—especially if you are forming a startup that you want to accelerate rapidly. But if you are going to do this, do it with intention. Choose the right people with the right skills at the right time. Do not, ever, choose to go into business with others because you don't think you are 'enough'. And do not bring people along who do not have the technical skills your startup needs because you want to help them out.

> *I am more than good enough.*

CO-FOUNDERS

Spend any time in an innovation space—whether on an accelerator program or working in a coworking space—and you will hear about co-founders. It seems to be super trendy these days to have co-founders. Not just that, but it almost seems to be expected. Anytime I have applied for a grant or an accelerator program, I've been asked to name my co-founders. And anytime I've been at a hackathon or similar, I've been part of a team. Further, angel investors at the Canberra Innovation Network have been frank: many, such as Nick McNaughton, rarely invest in startups that only have one founder.

An article by startup accelerator Startmate also makes the case for co-founders.[30] Startmate's courses include a Startmate founder program that is aimed at connecting people to form startups together. It also has a female fellowship program aimed at getting women ready to co-found or work at startups. The article quotes Rory San Miguel, co-founder of drone startup Propellor, as saying that a co-founder is essential. 'Don't do it alone,' he says. 'Just don't.' The article goes on to quote Alan Jin, co-founder of Muso, as saying that paying someone to do the work isn't always the answer. 'They [people in the ideation phase] don't realise you can't just pay someone to do something and then expect them to walk away. Whatever you've paid them to do needs to grow with you,' he says.

I was discussing how many founders a startup should have with Dr Craig Davis, GM Growth Programs at the Canberra Innovation Network. He said the conventional path is for startups to be made up of three co-founders—the hipster, the hacker and the hustler.

The hipster, hacker and hustler description was first coined by AKQA's chief technology officer Rei Inamoto in 2012, who used it to describe the basis for an effective dream team. The idea is that the hipster designs a product or service, the hacker builds it and the hustler sells it. The 'three co-founders' wisdom has led to many startups consciously seeking to have three people with different skills as part of the team.

CASE STUDY
Pearler

Pearler is a share-trading platform aimed at making it easy for people on the Financial Independence, Retire Early (FIRE) path—principally millennials and gen Z investors. The platform uses goal-tracking and automation features to make investing more about achieving what you want in life, rather than trading simply for profit. It also makes starting the investing journey fun and easy through following financial influencers, and real people who list their portfolios and approach to finance. (Note: I'm one such financial influencer.)

I first met the team at Pearler in 2019 when I was invited to participate on a panel they were putting together for the Sydney showing of the documentary Playing with FIRE. The team of three—Hayden Smith, Nick Nicolaides and Kurt Walkom—were part of the UNSW Founders Program.

Each of the co-founders performed different roles. Kurt handled much of the communication with financial influencers, and in the lead-up to the launch and immediately after it, I communicated with him more often. Hayden handled most of the technical details and was the person people spoke to regarding helpdesk queries (especially in the early days). And Nick was working full time at an investment-management firm during the early stages, so he dealt mainly with the institutional partners required to get a relatively unheard-of Pearler off the ground.

Pearler launched just as COVID hit in March 2020. I was the second external person to use the site and am also an early investor. After a year of testing, the platform was ready for public launch in early 2021. As of December 2021, Pearler has had over $200 million invested in shares and exchange-traded funds and its community continues to grow.

It makes sense to build a team that has a diversity of skill sets. I like writing, for instance, as well as public relations and social media. I'm comfortable participating in radio and television interviews, and I like being a podcast host. But I'm less technically minded, and I don't always pick up on details. Meanwhile, my husband is a technical officer in his day job and loves ICT. He edits my podcasts and is much better with detail (and more patient) than I am. But he's shy and doesn't like being behind the microphone.

> *I attract the right people to help my team grow.*

In her address during the online seminar for Women's Entrepreneurship Day (Australia and New Zealand) in 2021, entrepreneur and philanthropist Theresa Gattung CNZM said it makes sense to build a team when going into business, as it brings together different skill sets. She would know; she co-founded My Food Bag, New Zealand's longest-serving meal kit provider, with Cecilia Robinson and husband James Robinson, celebrity chef Nadia Lim, and Nadia's husband Carlos Bagrie.

CASE STUDY
Go-To

Zoë Foster Blake is another entrepreneur who has used co-founders to her advantage. Zoë is a former beauty writer and editor who came up with an idea for a skincare range. Now her Go-To range of products is a big hit with consumers and stocked at major beauty retailers. In August

2021, she agreed to sell 50.1% of her company, which netted her around $30 million.

In building Go-To, Zoë brought on three co-founders, including Stefan Drury (who helped her build her website), Peter Lehrke (who helped develop formulations) and Paul Bates (former managing director). 'I was very confident that I could create the products that I wished existed. I just didn't know how to practically do that,' she told The Australian Financial Review Magazine.[31]

In addition to bringing together people with the right skill sets for the startup, another advantage of the co-founder structure is that you have other people around to bounce ideas off. According to a Startmate article, 'it's often easier when you have a second set of eyes, or someone to share the load, or whatever cliché you want to employ.'[32]

My experience is that being a solopreneur can be lonely. No-one else seems to get what you are doing or what you are working on. And even creative people like me can find that they don't have the same diversity of thought that comes with working as part of a team. There is a certain buzz, or synergy, when you share an idea and then others in the group build on it to make it bigger and better.

But Craig disputes the notion that you need at least three co-founders. 'You don't need a co-founder for the sake of a co-founder,' he says. 'Some startups might have co-founders and others might have team members who are invested in other ways. And you might have a mix of roles—there is no formula for the right mix. The people you have onboard need to be part of the vision and be inspired by it.'

Having more than one co-founder could also, potentially, lead to organisational confusion. Business coach and CEO of Black Bull Performance Group Steve Gregory says that in his experience, people need clear leadership, and generally that means there can only be one person in charge. 'As humans, we look to our leaders to provide guidance and it's hard to have clear leadership when there is more than one leader,' he says.

I am a leader.

There is a famous Chinese proverb about three monks who lived in a temple on top of a mountain (三个和尚没水喝). At first, there was only one monk, who lived as a hermit and would walk down the mountain every day to fetch drinking water. When a second monk joined him, they would go down together. But when a third monk joined the temple, they squabbled over whose turn it was and they all went thirsty. The moral here is that having more people can reduce organisational efficiency—especially in terms of leadership.

Good communication between the co-founders is essential. Co-founder issues is one of the key reasons that startups fail—and co-founder relationships are something that potential investors will focus on.

CASE STUDY
Swipebucket and Swipebasket

If ever there was a story about what could go wrong with a partnership, then the startup Swipebucket is it. Swipebucket is a tool that enables users to capture information from a computer and save it for easy use later. For instance, if you read a great quote in an article and want to use it in your newsletter later, you can easily swipe it, save it and organise it.

Swipebucket was a partnership of three co-founders—Nicky (who had the original idea), Sankha (who did the coding) and Ursa. Nicky and Ursa are New Yorkers while Sankha is based in India. The app debuted on startup-tech site AppSumo and did well. One of my friends used it and found it easy and convenient to use.

One day, my friend noticed that the app had changed its name to Swipebasket. She then started receiving emails saying that Sankha had taken Swipebucket down, cloned it and moved the personal data of customers to Swipebasket. Sankha and his friends have a different story about what happened.

Whatever the truth is, the Swipebucket/basket case illustrates the problems that can happen with partnerships and co-founders—including where they are operating in different jurisdictions that can make legal remedies difficult.

COMPETITION WITH OTHERS

Attend any course about launching a business or startup, and you will hear about the need to check out the competition.

This can be a tricky thing for some startups. If you do some research and find no businesses in your niche, it can be easy to think, *Oh, no one is interested in this and there is no market.* But on the other hand, if you do some research and find there are masses of big companies doing what you had planned to do, you might then think, *Oh, well there are already others in this space—how could I compete with them?*

Both are manifestations of scarcity mindset and imposter syndrome. The thing is, your business or startup will reflect YOU. It will be unique. It will solve a problem in different ways. And just because it has been done before, doesn't mean it can't be done better.

Just think of Uber. There was a time when it was the only player in the rideshare space. But now there is Ola, Lyft, Shebah and many others. Sometimes, the first mover doesn't end up being the market leader. Think of how BlackBerry has been overtaken by the iPhone, Skype is being eclipsed by Zoom, and online accounting programs like MYOB being outshone by Xero.

When I started my first blog—a review blog of food and places in Taiwan called *Taiwanxifu*—I did a quick Google search and came up with a site called *A Hungry Girl's Guide to Taipei*. She seemed to have nailed it: many foodie places were on there, and most expats told me about her site. How could I compete? I was so tempted at first to just give up and not even try.

But after I had been in Taipei for a few months, I decided to go ahead and launch it. While I included reviews of a lot of expat places similar to Hungry Girl, over time, I developed a different niche. Hungry Girl was an American woman of Asian heritage; in Taiwan, she craved food from home like burgers. I was an Australian woman married to a Taiwanese man. I went to a lot of high-end places for work functions, but my real love was Taiwanese street food and culture. I began to write more and more, not just about food, but about the cultural connection. And when I had a baby in Taiwan, I even blogged about my experience of being locked up for a month in post-baby confinement.

I'm sharing this because it's important to be aware of the competition, but then turn a blind eye, trust your intuition, and do it anyway.

Career and business coach Bec McFarland shares that she never researched who her 'competitors' were before starting. 'I've never really been aware of the competition in my business,' she says. 'People used to ask me about what other career coaches there were out there. But I was more focused on what I wanted to achieve so I didn't spend the time and energy looking at my competitors. All of my time, energy, love, and attention went to grow my own business—not anyone else's.'

Bec identifies being too focused on competitors as a form of scarcity mindset. 'When we are focused on what our competitors are doing, then we come from a place of worry about lack,' she says. 'We are then closing ourselves off to receiving the opportunity to grow our own business.'

I relate to this scarcity/abundance thinking. As a personal finance writer, I'm not worried about there being other books out there about how to save money and invest. When people become interested in personal finance, they often want to read everything in the genre. I've now met many financial influencers and people in the FIRE movement. We share similar values and several have shared their wisdom on my podcast. I don't feel threatened by their books or podcasts; instead, I feel like I am part of a community.

Bec says business owners, especially in the coaching space, often become worried about others 'stealing' their clients. 'Everyone has their own free will and capability to choose where they spend their money,' says Bec. 'Stealing clients doesn't exist. We all need to hear things from different voices. It's the way we learn and develop. If we just learnt from one person, we would all just be the same and there would not be an opportunity for growth, development, innovation, continuous improvement and diversity of thought.'

Related to this is the fear of others stealing ideas from you. This can often lead to people being scared to put out information or products because they are worried others will copy them. On this, Bec is blunt: 'Are you going to keep yourself small and keep your ideas to yourself and not share something that could potentially help another human being because you are worried someone else is going to copy you?' she says. 'Focus on keeping in your own lane and being on your own journey.

There is only one Bec: I'm not worried about someone else copying me.'

COLLABORATION AND CO-CREATION

Being in a partnership or co-founder relationship has certain risks. And I tend to be quite cautious when it comes to entering into formal partnerships.

But that doesn't mean that I don't like cooperating with other people. I love collaboration and co-creating with other people, and I believe that working with and helping others in business can be one of the most beneficial things you can do. But it's important to do it in the right way.

Bec McFarland says we can often dive in full blast and go, 'Let's do this thing—we can go into partnership with each other.' But collaborations often fail because there isn't an alignment of values or work ethic. 'You can end up with one person doing all the work and the other person not pulling their weight,' she says. 'Accordingly, I don't recommend going out to start up a whole bunch of businesses with different people all at once.'

But collaborations and co-creation can be really useful. Unlike a partnership, you retain your brand identity. You come together often for a particular project or event. It allows you to work with people who have different skill sets and you can cross-promote each other's businesses.

Another reason for being involved in collaboration is socialisation.

'As a solopreneur, it can be really isolating,' says Bec. 'A lot of my clients struggle because they feel like they are on their own. And often that community vibe, collaboration and working on a similar objective can be so rewarding.'

Business advisor Janine Linklater also agrees that there can be value in collaboration. 'I'm seeing a lot of clients come in with ideas for creative collaborations that are not partnerships,' she says.

ORGANISATIONAL STRUCTURE

Even if you are a solopreneur starting out, it's important to think about your team.

Who do you have on your team? It could be your spouse, bookkeeper, lawyer, house cleaner, copywriter, website developer, business coach, podcast editor or dog walker. You might not have many people on your team—yet—but if you want to grow, it's important to think about who else you might need.

Just because you don't have formal partners, doesn't mean you can't have a team. And it doesn't mean that your team all have to be sitting in an office, with you lording over them as founder and CEO. These days, it's increasingly easy to hire virtual assistants who can work remotely—and for as little or as long as you need them to.

EXERCISES

1.

If you were to bring on a partner or co-founder,
who would it be?
(a) Why? What strengths or attributes
would they bring?

2.

How do you envisage your business growing? Do
you want it to be big? Or remain small?
(a) How would you resolve an issue with a partner
who holds a different vision?

3.

Who is currently on your team? List everyone from
a spouse/partner to cleaners, bookkeepers, lawyers,
gardeners or childcare centres.

4.

What skills or attributes will you need in your
business as it grows?

9
SUPER PRODUCTIVITY

This is not a chapter about coaching you to be a superwoman.

While I think the outfit is sexy, it doesn't quite fit me. And beyond the bling, there is a real problem with people, especially women, burning themselves out trying to do too much.

This is, however, a chapter that contains practical and mental tips for maximising your time, being super productive and freeing yourself to focus on your business.

'How do you do so much?' I get asked this all the time, usually by other women wanting to know the mystical secret. I'm unusual in that I like being busy, despite it not always being healthy. But there are times when I need to slow down and do less. Life is not a competition for doing more.

I suffer from anxiety and perfectionism, and at times it's a real problem. Part of it stems from worrying about being perceived as lazy. I've learnt to let go of this; it's another way of telling myself that I am not good enough.

> *I do not need to work hard to prove I'm good enough.*

Conversations about needing to 'work hard' to be successful concern me. Certainly, it's important to have a good work ethic. But the need to 'work hard'—rather than to work productively, collaboratively, intuitively, respectfully and purposely—is problematic.

For women, the fear of not working hard enough can be especially toxic, and lead to poor physical and mental wellbeing. And when you think about it, even the Bible urges us to take a break at least one day a week.

BISY BACKSON

Have you ever noticed that when people greet each other, the first thing they do is talk about how busy they are?

I remember learning Mandarin Chinese in the early 1990s. There was this sentence pattern in my textbook:

'How are you? Are you busy/not busy?'

'I'm very busy. And you?'

'I'm also very busy.'

I remember laughing so hard at this! Where was the polite 'How are you going?' It seemed so alien. But these days, the 'I'm busy' formula has somehow crept in to all aspects of our social interactions in modern Australia. Not only that, but it's become almost a competition when meeting and greeting other people. I see it as part of the cult of business.

There's a big problem with this. Sometimes, we are so busy running around doing things that we overlook the obvious, or we spend time doing things that don't need to be done. In the book *The Tao of Pooh*,[33] which explains Taoism (aka Daoism) in a fun way, Rabbit goes off on a wild-goose chase looking for the Tao, not realising it is a philosophical construct. He leaves a note saying *Bisy backson* (i.e. *Busy, back soon*), and won't stop for anyone. I can so relate to this; so often I have been too busy running around, trying to find something, create something or do something, that I don't listen to others who have the answer. Or I have not realised that I knew the answer or had what I was looking for all along.

How often have you run around doing things to appear productive rather than produce the outcomes you wanted to focus on? Sometimes, doing things is a form of procrastination. If you've ever studied for an exam or written a book, you will understand how hard it can be to ignore a sudden urge to clean the fridge or mow the lawn. Anything, in fact, other than doing the task at hand.

It's important to do some strategic work around identifying visions, goals and tasks so that we can organise our time. It's not that we are lazy (usually far from it). But when we are unsure of what to do, it's easy to get distracted by the other tasks (especially 'shiny objects'), overcommit to the expectations of others, overwork and do too much—or the opposite: wallow in self-doubt, overwhelm or indecision.

JUST MAKE THE DECISION

One of the biggest blockers to productivity is failing to make a decision.

For instance, in 2021 I spent weeks deciding whether to cancel Women's Entrepreneurship Day due to COVID or pivot to an online event. I hesitated and waited and put my head in the sand until the last possible minute. I knew the decision I needed to make—I even knew the answer—but it took me weeks of overthinking before I got there.

Failing to make a decision not only wastes time but can also demoralise your team. Who likes having a boss who can't make decisions? Does it make you feel as if your boss trusts and values you? Nup. Failure to make a decision, especially when you have all the information, is a sign of poor leadership.

Related to this, failure to make a decision is a decision. While life can get busy, if you put off making a decision, you have made a decision *not* to make a decision. You are effectively saying no but not owning it. You might think you have sidestepped the decision, but people know. People notice.

> *I trust my intuition. I have the right information
> to make a good decision.*

BEING IN FLOW

Have you ever been so immersed in thinking about a task that you lose track of time or jump out of your skin when someone comes up to you? When I'm deep in the writing zone, I can be like that.

There's been a lot written about the importance of flow, and you usually get into the flow state when you are working in your creative, genius zone. Of course, you can't be in your flow state all the time. Imagine if all you did was write all day and then forgot to pick up the kids from school, pay the bills, respond to urgent emails or feed the pets? There are a lot of things to juggle and that's half the problem.

> *My business and I are in harmony and flow.*

But the converse is true: if all you did all day was housework and caring for others, you wouldn't have time for your passion project. Are you making space in your life to do the important things you are called to do? How are you carving out time to have quiet, uninterrupted flow?

My mother, who was a fashion designer for many years, gets up before dawn, makes herself an espresso and sketches. It's in this pre-dawn time when no-one else is up that she is in her flow zone of creativity and productivity.

Bec Cuzzillo from the Spiritual Business Academy talks about overcoming limiting beliefs like *I need to work really hard*. Instead, she recommends embracing the feminine way of doing business, which is more about ease, grace and flow. According to Bec, while the masculine energy is important for ensuring we take action to make things happen, 'if we're just stuck in that space we are just doing, doing, doing, whereas the feminine space is more around being.'

Bec shares that her experience in a traditional workplace has been of working according to a clock—and those hours could be productive, or not. The hours remain the same, but productivity changes on any given day. 'When you work for yourself and especially if you've got children and you're doing all of your work within nap times, then those hours count,' she says. 'You've got to be productive in those hours.'

THE JUGGLING ACT

Women wear a lot of hats—especially if they have kids. The mental load of remembering everything from Book Week to play dates and the perfect present for your mother-in-law can be almost as wearing as the physical housework. If you add an expectation that you should be working crazy-long hours as well, it's a recipe for disaster.

Bec Cuzzillo notes that often the model of 'male successful business owner who works hard and plays hard' relies on the fact that he is not the primary carer of his children. Often, women are juggling being entrepreneurs, caregivers, homemakers—all of those roles. 'Even if you have a partner that you share a lot with, there is still a burden of responsibilities that plays out in your heart,' she says. Bec is big on designing our lives and businesses in a way that supports us to have all of those parts working in balance.

Feminine energy is, as she describes it, more about working with the seasons. For instance, if you are a mum with young children, you may do less (or even take a break from work and business for a while). But then later in life, you may build on what you have done earlier and do more.

Being honest about the juggling act and resulting time limitations can help you make different choices. In the case of Bec, when she had her son, she restructured her business to move away from one-on-one coaching towards group coaching, which allows her to spend more time with her son and also spread her message and magic with a bigger group of people.

MULTITASKING DOESN'T WORK

In our modern life, we have become adept at multitasking. I would also argue that many women are intuitive multitaskers; we're used to looking after kids while cooking dinner and talking on the phone. Blinging, beeping smartphones and constant messages on different apps further disrupt our thinking.

But we're being effective and getting even more done, right? Wrong. We are *slower* at doing tasks when we multitask. We might think we are doing several things at once, but actually, we are switching back and forward, leading to 'task switch costs'—i.e. the negative effects of task switching, such as increased mental demand from our thoughts jumping around.[34]

In addition, we are more likely to make mistakes when our focus is shifting.[35] This is why it's never a good idea to speak (or even worse—text) on a mobile phone while driving—and why it's illegal to hold your phone to speak or text while driving.

Extending that to our business, it's easy to get distracted—especially when we are doing something that is hard, requires concentration or is unpleasant. Even while writing this chapter, I was super tempted to multitask by checking multiple Facebook messages. But each time I gave into temptation, my attention wandered just that little bit and it made it harder for me to return to my train of thought.

CHUNKING TIME

One of the barriers to getting started is, well, just getting started. The other barrier is getting distracted and falling for multitasking. On this, there are a few timing hacks that can force you to get started.

- **The Pomodoro Technique.** This is perhaps one of the most famous systems. Named after a tomato-shaped oven timer (note: I'm on the lookout for these at op shops—I so want one), it involves using a timer and working for twenty-five minutes (with a five-minute break). After four pomodoros, you then have a longer break of fifteen to twenty minutes.[36]

- **The 20-minute dash.** If you are procrastinating or feeling anxious, a good technique is to set your timer for twenty minutes and just see how much work you can get done. This short period isn't too daunting; it's not all day and it's just a teaser. But it's super effective at getting you started. I used this effectively when doing some administrative tasks in my public service role that were complex; without the discipline of this method, it was hard to get started and even harder to stay focused.

- **Fifty-two and seventeen.** According to a study done by productivity app DeskTime, ten per cent of the most productive people have a specific formula: they work for fifty-two minutes and then rest for seventeen.[37] I've been doing a form of it for years, although not always with a timer. I find when writing that twenty minutes isn't enough to focus my mind, but that an hour is too long. Fifty-two minutes is just right.

Try some of these methods and see what works for you. There is no right or wrong—but these simple timing tricks can help you to focus your mind and boost productivity.

> *I am focused and productive.*

PROJECT MANAGING YOURSELF

Maybe you are a super organised, proactive and motivated person. So am I (most of the time). But being in an office and having a boss tell you what to do and when to do it by and having people around you who remind you when it is lunchtime and time to go home is one thing. Working by yourself, at home, with only yourself to remind you about what you 'should' be working on and when is another thing.

Most people find managing themselves hard, and I'm no exception. I can vacillate between working fifteen-hour days and not getting enough sleep, to feeling listless and lacking in purpose and unsure what to do next.

And for those balancing a startup with full- or part-time work, it can be even harder. Once you get home, it's easy just to relax and kick back, and then before you know it, the day has gone.

> *I am productive, organised and efficient.*

Thankfully, I've developed a few hacks and techniques to manage my time and keep me motivated. Here are some of the tools I recommend.

1. **Google Calendar.** I schedule all of my appointments in Google Calendar. I don't agree to anything until I check there first. I like that it is easy to access the calendar both on my phone and on my computer, and these days, most events will give you an option to share to your Google Calendar. I can also schedule times to work on things that will increase my efficiency (like writing).

2. **An online project-management tool.** I'm going to talk about this in more detail shortly. Finding a good online project-management tool that works for you is gold. It's like lifting a weight off your shoulders. And if you're in an 'I don't know what to do next' funk, or you have an unexpected ten or fifteen minutes between meetings, you have a list of ready items to access.

3. **A paper diary.** I like to go digital where possible—especially for managing appointments—but I still love my paper diary. Choosing my annual diary is a bit of a ritual, and I especially like a diary that is uplifting and inspiring, and allows me to include a pen. I use my paper diary for thinking about my monthly and weekly goals and writing down my daily to-do lists. I like to take it with me if I know I'm going to a cafe to meet someone. That way, if I get there early—or if they're late—I can sit and work

through my tasks. Using a ruler, I divide each day in half. On the left side, I write work-related tasks. And on the right, I write home-related tasks. I'm impossibly ambitious, but I have found that generally I accomplish three to four things a day maximum.

4. **Post-it notes.** Sometimes I get my best ideas at random times, like when I'm working on an article that requires focus, or an urgent task in my day job. When this happens, I write it down on a Post-it note. I could put these items directly into a project-management tool on my phone or computer, but sometimes, I find myself going down a rabbit warren (*I'll just read this on Facebook, just respond to this SMS ... oooh, I wonder what is happening on Instagram*). If I'm having an especially busy day at work, I will just stick the Post-it note onto my smartphone and then when I return home after dinner, transcribe it into my paper diary or project-management tool.

5. **A sheet of paper.** Some days, I'm feeling anxious and my thoughts are scatty. I feel like I need to do everything now and I can't prioritise. The risk is I run around doing half of one thing and a bit of another, and not finish anything. For these occasions, I make myself a hot cup of tea and sit down with a piece of paper and a bright pen. Sometimes (being a frugalista), I will use the back of a used envelope. It doesn't matter. I do a brain dump of EVERYTHING I think I need to do. I then pick three top items, and write them neatly in my diary or (if I think they are more substantive) put them in my online project-management tool. I then mentally ignore the rest and focus on these three. I know I will get to the others; I'm just prioritising these first.

It's also worth aligning your weekly tasks to your strategic goals. Remember that business plan you did with yearly, three-yearly and five-yearly goals? How is what you are doing day to day aligning with that? Plans do go astray, and shiny objects are distracting. But it's worth checking what you are spending your time on against what you want to accomplish.

THE IMPORTANCE OF PROJECT MANAGEMENT

Why have a project-management tool? If you've ever organised an event or managed a project—even if it was your wedding—you will know how many little and big things there are to do. And if you're working with others, it's important to assign roles and share updates so that you can work as a team.

An easy and often effective project-management tool is a document. You can use an Excel spreadsheet, and even have it available in Google Drive, Dropbox, Box or another app to share with other users.

I like to make a simple table, like the example of the Christmas lunch matrix.

Christmas Lunch

Date Due	Description	Comments	Responsibility
~~01/10~~	~~Make plum pudding~~		~~Sarah~~
01/12	Agree on venue	Hoping someone else will host this year	Mum
02/12	Send out invitations	Create a Facebook event?	Mum
12/12	Confirm the list of attendees		Mum
15/12	Draft menu		Mary
20/12	Purchase ham		Dad
25/12	Set up trestle tables		Tom

I'm guessing most families aren't quite this organised for Christmas lunch (we're not), but you can see how effective this method can be. I used to include a fifth column (Done, yes/no), but these days, I just strike through the items. You can also highlight items if you want to draw attention to them—e.g. because it needs more work.

Once you set it out like this, it becomes obvious if only one person is doing the lion's share of tasks (often, it's you). Just think how often Mum ends up doing everything at Christmas, for starters! And then there are all the little things that need to be done, but you kind of forget about: wrapping presents, buying bonbons (unless you are adopting a more sustainable alternative), chilling the sparkling wine, beer and soft drinks. If you have a list like this, you are more likely to remember things. You can also do an accompanying budget, which could help make sure you don't go into debt.

The other advantage to using a project-management tool is that you have a record of what to do next time. For instance, my Zonta club has a number of regular activities, including the Pre-loved Fashion Sale and the Zonta Says NO campaign that runs during the 16 Days of Global Activism against Gender-Based Violence. Having a project-management list means that we don't need to reinvent the wheel from one year to the next. It's clear who coordinated the invitations, who did floral displays in the libraries, and who designed the flyers.

How many things do you work on where there are multiple moving parts? Could a project-management list help you stay focused across each project and/or task?

ONLINE PROJECT-MANAGEMENT TOOLS

If you are working on a larger project, or just want to organise your thoughts into tasks and priorities in a more intentional way, there are a range of online management tools that can help. Note that I don't have an affiliate relationship with any of these products. You will need to investigate and find out what works best for you.

CHECKLISTS

An online checklist is a bit like having an online shopping list: it can help you remember all those bits and pieces you might otherwise forget. It's a simple project-management tool, but it can still be effective.

There are numerous digital checklists available, including:

- **Google Tasks.** A good thing about this list is that you can enter it onto a Android smartphone and it is therefore transportable wherever you go.

- **Microsoft To Do.** Microsoft has developed a handy checklist function. If you are using Microsoft 365, you may already have it.

PROJECT-MANAGEMENT TOOLS

There are several online project-management tools, and it feels like more are hitting the market every day. Many of the newer ones are intuitive to use and great for working on projects across teams.

- **Asana.** I fell in love with Asana. When I discovered it, I thought, *Where has this been all my life?* However, while it brought me joy, it was also the most expensive option that I researched for teamwork and sadly, we broke up.

- **Zoho Projects.** As I was already using Zoho, I moved to their Zoho Projects. It is similar to Asana, but to be honest, I was on the rebound. One feature it has that I like is the timer function. It is also (at the time of writing) free to use for up to three users. As I have a Zoho One membership, it is already part of the suite of apps I have.

- **monday.com.** This program is becoming increasingly popular, and is being advertised heavily. It is similar to Asana and uses bright colours to track workloads across a team.

- **Trello.** Based on a Kanban card system, Trello is a great way to track the progress of tasks by moving cards along a pipeline. Recently, long-time advocates have been moving away from it due to cost increases. But do try it and see if it meets your needs.

AUTOMATION

One way to be more efficient is to automate some of your key tasks. For instance, in the past, I used to spend lots of time going back and forward with podcast guests, trying to organise a time, research information about them and then ask them for photos. Now, when I'm talking to someone about being a guest on *The Joyful Frugalista* podcast, I give them a link to my online booking calendar in Zoho. They choose a time that suits them, book it in, and then they get an email back with information about the podcasting process and a link to a Zoho form (where they can provide their information and upload a preferred photo).

Anyone can set up automations, even if you're not especially computer savvy. According to Sheree Henley, who I featured in a Facebook Live interview on automations, the hardest step is thinking through your business systems and understanding your business flows. She recommends keeping a notebook and recording all tasks you do regularly over two weeks, then seeing what you could automate. She uses a program called Keap to automate a funnel of selling webinars and memberships.

COWORKING

COVID has shown that while some people love working from home, others (like me) suffer from feeling isolated. I thought I would love working from home by myself, but I have realised I enjoy socialising with others. Thankfully, you can re-create the feeling of being in an office without having an office job through coworking.

PHYSICAL COWORKING SPACES

The rise in entrepreneurship has seen a corresponding rise in coworking spaces. It works like this: you find a space that suits you, you work out whether you want to be there full- or part-time, and you pay for a membership. Usually, a coworking space will have desks, chairs, power points for your laptop, WiFi, meeting rooms, a kitchenette, and sometimes beverages for TGIF or other occasions.

While people in the coworking space will be working on their projects and you need to be mindful of noise (a bit like being in a library), just being in a space with others can often create synergies. You never know who you will meet in the kitchenette, or bond with over morning tea. I cowork one day a week at the Canberra Innovation Network, and I love the positive vibes of being there. It's only a fifteen-minute walk from home, and whenever I go there, I come back recharged and inspired.

VIRTUAL COWORKING

Another option is a virtual coworking space. You can set this up with entrepreneurial friends or as part of a group. You meet up online (e.g. on Zoom), you chat for a bit about your goals for the session, and then you put Zoom on mute and go off and do your own thing. The discipline of knowing that other people are online working at the same time can force you to stay focused, avoid multitasking and get in the zone. It's a great way to do things like finish writing a book or work on a new proposal.

I'm currently part of a virtual writing coworking space run by author and editor Kellie Nissen from Just Right Words. Yes, I could just write by myself (and I often do). But knowing there is someone at the end of a Zoom chat helps me focus and stay motivated to finish the task at hand.

Have you joined The Joyful Business Club Facebook group? I run regular virtual coworking sessions and also regular Facebook Lives on business-related topics. It's a great way to build connections, stay motivated and keep on track.

OUTSOURCING

When you are new in business, it's easy to fall into the trap of doing everything yourself. I'm a frugalista, so I like to reduce my start-up costs. I also like to learn new things, including how to set up new automations, basic website design, and so on.

The problem is that when you are not operating in your zone of genius, it takes a lot more time. You probably won't do as good a job as professionals who love what they do, either.

Business adviser Janine Linklater regularly teaches about the dangers of failing to outsource. If you think of what your business is and how much you can earn doing it, are you wasting money by doing too much DIY? For instance, I do most of my bookkeeping, but I missed out on some JobKeeper payments because I (erroneously) thought I was ineligible. Once I hired a bookkeeper, she immediately told me to apply—and helped me crunch the numbers. That was money well spent.

EXAMPLE: THE BENEFITS OF OUTSOURCING
**Janine Linklater provides an example of
how outsourcing can save you money**

Let's say paying an independent bookkeeper costs $100 per hour plus GST. On the face of it that is an additional expense for a small start-up business to incorporate—I get it.

Now let's say your time is valued at $50 per hour based on an annual salary of about $99,000. If you take on average four hours per week to complete your bookkeeping, that's $200 per week, or $10,400 per year.

A qualified bookkeeper can probably get your work done one day per month (or often less, but let's be conservative), which equates to $800 per month or $9,600 per year. This saves some money compared to if you did it yourself, and ... and this is the biggy ...

Imagine if you had those four hours per week back. What could that mean for your business? You could choose to focus on what you do best—engaging in business growth activities such as selling your product or service. For example, if you have a business that provides quotes for work, you could be keeping these up to date or making follow-up calls and getting more paying customers through the door.

What if just one of those quotes was for a $20,000, $50,000 or $100,000 job? If you're putting off this type of work to 'do the books' (or for that matter, any other administrative work that can be outsourced or delegated), how much income are you potentially missing out on by not focusing your energy where it is best utilised?

And if you don't do it regularly and it builds up to a point that you are late with your ATO lodgements, don't forget to add their late payment fees and fines as well as the accountant fees that you will incur into your actual costs.

I am good at delegating.

VIRTUAL ASSISTANTS

The working-from-home revolution has enabled many people to start up new businesses working as virtual assistants (VAs). Essentially, a VA works like a secretary or admin support, but they may do anything from setting up automations, to writing newsletters, bookkeeping, social media, organising webinars and creating sales funnels.

Blogger Michelle of *FrugalityandFreedom* was working in New Zealand as an events manager—until COVID hit. She returned to her hometown of Adelaide in March 2020 and pivoted to work as a VA, especially with financial influencers (finfluencers). As she has a strong stable of contacts in that field, she easily found work doing everything from editing and organising an ebook to podcast production.

Working with a good VA who has specialist skills can revolutionise your life. I currently have a VA (the lovely Susan Basiaco from *The Social Nest*) who designs and schedules social media for *The Joyful Fashionista*. In the past, I've had someone write my newsletter, and as my businesses grow, hiring VAs with specialist skills may be easier and quicker than hiring full-time staff.

EXERCISES

1.
What habits or mindset blocks are preventing you from operating as productively as you could?
For instance, do you have trouble saying no, or are you spending too much time reading clickbait or responding to Facebook messenger conversations?

2.
Are you giving yourself enough rest and self-care? What could you do now to allow yourself some time away from your business?

3.
Are you engaging in too much multitasking? Dedicate a time when you can do your work without social media interruptions. You can even mute some social media for a while, or subscribe to a program that can do it for you.

4.
Explore different project-management tools and try one to see if it suits you.

5.
What repetitive and time-consuming tasks are you doing that could be automated or outsourced? Keep a list for fourteen days of all the tasks you do, then review and take action as appropriate.

6.
Attend a coworking centre, sign up for a virtual coworking session or make a coworking date with a friend.

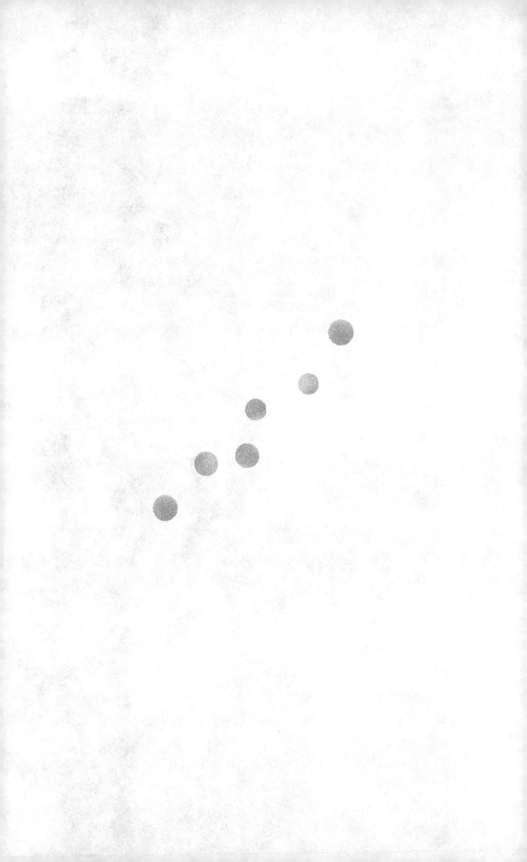

10
READY, SET, LAUNCH!

Launching your business or a new product is super exciting—yet also scary. In this chapter, I will share a few ideas to help your new venture take off and grow.

FEAR OF SUCCESS

Have you heard of fear of failure? Well, what about fear of success? It's a thing.

When we are successful at something, our relationships with people around us change. Some people will be super happy for us, while others will feel threatened. You are disrupting the status quo. How dare you go and follow your dreams and be more successful than they are?

If you have come from an abusive background, or are currently in it, you may on some level have taught yourself how to dull your shine around others. People with narcissistic tendencies don't want you to succeed; although they might not come out and say it, they will disrupt in their subtle ways.

It is safe to shine.

What this means is that we may have often socialised ourselves into rejecting success. It is one thing to dream about an exciting new venture and quite another thing to lean in and do it.

Ahead of the launch of *The Joyful Frugalista,* I started to get anxious. *What if this is a flop?* I started asking myself while sending my publisher emails about (non-existent) problems and issues. I was getting jittery and was even half thinking of stopping the book launch altogether. I always remember the kind words of one of the staff at my publisher. 'Relax. You have a well-written book, and it will do well,' she said.

That book launch week was amazing. I was on TV and radio stations nationally, including *Sunrise* and ABC Radio National Drive. I was so proud to be able to share my message, and it was so validating that people got it. I would never have had that experience if I had pulled out due to fear.

Can you relate to wanting to pull the pin on something exciting just as it's about to happen?

I permit myself to celebrate the success of my launch.

DON'T WAIT UNTIL YOUR PRODUCT IS PERFECT

Often, we want things to be perfect before we think it is good enough to launch. Or before we tell anyone about things. As I was writing this, I couldn't help but have Fairground Attraction's song 'Perfect' running through my head. *It's got to be peeerrfect.*

Before you can launch a product, it has to be safe. It is unethical and illegal to sell products or services you know are unsafe. You also need to ensure your products meet licensing and regulatory requirements, especially for food and healthcare items.

But here's the thing: it doesn't have to be perfect.

The more you do what you do, the better it will get. And sometimes, it's about being in the market in a timely way to meet customer demand. Too perfect and too late means you will have missed the moment and competitors will have an advantage.

CASE STUDY
Microsoft

Ever heard of a little company called Microsoft? What you probably don't realise about Microsoft is that it's a case study in going ahead and revolutionising the software industry—before it was ready.

These days, Microsoft products are known for being trustworthy. But I remember a time when their products were glitchy. There was even a joke going around (way before self-driving cars were a thing) about how if Microsoft developed a car, you would have to shut down and reboot it all the time. Yet Microsoft's lack of perfection didn't stop it from becoming a key player in the emerging personal computer industry.

Paul Allen and Bill Gates founded Microsoft in 1977, with Gates famously leaving Harvard University to join the company. In 1980, personal computers were virtually unheard of. IBM was working on a secret program called Project Chess, which aimed to develop a personal computer that could be used by most people (not just computer-science programmers working in big computer rooms). IBM had been cautious about diving into computing. It usually developed products in-house, but decided to outsource to move quickly, as it wanted to capture the personal computer market. It approached Microsoft, and Gates attended a meeting with IBM executives. There he convinced IBM that Microsoft could develop a disk operating system (DOS).[38] The rest is history.

The interesting thing about this story is that Microsoft was not the frontrunner. Gates suggested another firm, Digital Research Inc (DRI), and according to some reports, Gates called DRI's founder during a meeting with IBM, as Gates felt DRI had more experience. While Microsoft was a market leader in several coding languages, DRI was then the leading supplier of computer operating systems. But DRI founder Gary Kildall did not sign the deal with IBM; Microsoft did. There are conflicting accounts of why this occurred. Some say Kildall would not sign IBM's non-disclosure agreement and others say that he was away on a trip and the IBM deal wasn't a priority.[39]

Whatever the story, the takeaway is that Microsoft saw an opportunity, and even though Allen and Gates felt they were not ready, they seized it. At that point, they had no experience developing computer operating systems (not many people did), yet they undertook to do so. As Allen recounted in Idea Man: A Memoir by the Co-founder of Microsoft, 'thanks to a fluke … we'd been handed the opportunity to create the pivotal product of the era.'[40]

IBM paid Microsoft USD430,000 for the MS-DOS system. But that wasn't the main source of Microsoft's income from the deal. A provision in the agreement allowed Microsoft to license the operating system to other computer manufacturers, in effect separating the software from the hardware. This enabled Microsoft to sell its product to other computer manufacturers (and even home users), allowing it to become the dominant tech company of the era. Microsoft's revenue grew from USD16 million in 1981 to USD140 million in 1985.[41]

> *I free myself from the need to be perfect.*
> *I learn as I grow.*

PRE-SELLING YOUR PRODUCT OR SERVICES

Here's the thing: you don't have to have your product ready before you sell it. Yep, you don't have to physically have something before it is ready.

I've successfully pitched book proposals to publishers without a completed manuscript (for non-fiction books, an excerpt is acceptable). And many of my blog readers and people in my community pre-purchased *The Joyful Frugalista* before it was launched. My publisher encouraged me to do so, as indie bookstores and others will often make purchasing decisions based on the volume of pre-orders.

Personal and business coach Wendy Marman sold dozens of copies of her leadership book before it hit the printer. What I loved about this was that not only was I, as a buyer, supporting her, but she sent me a lovely card telling me how much she valued my support. I have heard her speak many times and know that she will have a lot of wisdom to share. I'm looking forward to reading it.

International sales and networking coach Misty Henkel—who sold over one hundred copies of her first book, *Overcoming Obscurity: How to get noticed in the marketplace so that you can make more money* before publication—started selling her second book as she began to write it. At the time of writing, she has sold over twenty copies—and the book isn't finished. She aims to pay for the cost of the book through pre-selling alone.

According to Misty, an idea is easier to sell than a physical product. 'Once we get our hands on the ACTUAL product, the volume of stock can loom at us and we can begin to feel that we have a lot of work to do to sell it all. Without evidence that we can sell it, it can be difficult to get the motivation or courage to start peddling our wares in the marketplace.' Conversely, if you have already pre-sold items, you have evidence that they can be sold and it feels more like running a race downhill than uphill.

It works for products as well as books. Angie Rassi pre-sold her beautiful *Find Your Bling* personal-development board game. I purchased the $250 board game sight unseen in mid-2020 during COVID lockdown. With global supply-chain issues, her game did not arrive in Australia until early 2021, months after she had anticipated it would be ready. Did I feel ripped off? Not at all. Angie kept me updated about developments, and she created a hype around the game arriving. I was excited when she hand-delivered her beautiful silver-boxed game filled with jewels and cards with special messages. She recorded short videos with us all receiving them, which she shared on her socials.

Pre-selling also works especially well for courses. Rather than going to the trouble of developing a course and *then* selling it, some people first put a call out for those who are interested. For instance, you could do a Facebook Live or a Facebook challenge, and then at the end say, 'Who's interested in a course on [XYZ]? Type in the comments below or fill out this form to be on the waitlist.' Once you have sufficient interest, it will give you the confidence to proceed. Most online course platforms even have a built-in function allowing people to be on a waitlist or pre-launch.

If you regularly attend networking events, pre-selling is relatively easy. People will know you, trust you, and have a good idea about your work and what you do. You may even have an opportunity to pitch what you are doing so that you can actively pre-sell.

As outlined in Chapter 7, there are also online crowdfunding platforms that allow you to sell your product while it is still in the start-up phase. One of the best known of these is Kickstarter, whose mission is to 'help bring creative products to life'. Startups can list their product or project and ask the community for backing. As you might expect, Kickstarter tends to attract some amazing and innovative projects. At the time of writing, Kickstarter said that on that day it had funded forty-one projects, with USD1,666,086 raised.

An advantage of pre-selling is that it provides proof of concept. How do you know if people want to buy your product? And how do you mitigate the risk of spending a fortune in production, only for people not to buy it? Raising money via pre-sales to customers who already want the product can be a good strategy.

Of course, it is fraudulent to ask for money for a product that you don't plan to create. You need to be mindful that in asking for money from people you know (and don't), you are committing to deliver. Whether you are raising money on Kickstarter, or pre-selling through your social media community or networking group, be sure to be upfront about any details or problems and communicate regularly about progress.

MAKE IT EASY FOR PEOPLE TO PAY YOU

Make sure to create a page on your website that makes it easy for people to buy your product. You may be surprised how hard it can be to pay people sometimes. You want people to be able to buy with the click of a few buttons—one if possible. Ideally, you want to have a proper ecommerce solution on your website/s, such as WooCommerce or Shopify, or at least a program that manages inventory. If you are selling a large amount of stock, you will need a professional system for managing it.

But if you are starting small in an imperfect-action way, it may be enough just to give people your bank account details so that they can deposit funds straight away. While I usually trust those I know through networking and other channels to do the right thing, I don't usually publish my bank account details online. I now have a PayID account, which means that when I give people the code, they can deposit easily into my bank account. A bonus is that the money is transferred instantly. PayPal also makes it easy; all you need is an email address for people to transfer funds, but the platform also makes it easy to create a button (which you can put onto your website or social media), or even a QR code that people can scan.

> *I gratefully receive money in exchange for the value I give through my product or service.*

THE PERFECT LAUNCH PLAN

Here's the thing: there is no such thing as a perfect launch plan. You can hire a publicist, PR company or marketing team, and they'll come up with lots of ideas for you around things like events, paid media and earnt media. But ultimately, launching is about marketing your product—and often yourself as well. And marketing is often about understanding your target market, trying new things and having an innovative mindset. Most of all, it's about having a call to action as part of your messaging.

When I was preparing for the launch of *The Joyful Fashionista*, I created a spreadsheet and recorded all the thought bubbles I had. It's easier to do this when you're in a positive mood, dreaming about the future and possibilities, than when you are stressing and worrying about how to launch an existing product (the same logic as pre-selling). You could create a scrapbook if you are more visual. And make sure to notice what others in your field are doing. While I do not suggest you copy anyone else, you may be able to tweak or refine your strategy based on what you observe, in ways that feel right with you.

A successful launch is often made up of lots of little things rather than one big splash. In his book *The Success Principles: How to get from where you are to where you want to be*, Jack Canfield talks about the marketing for his book *Chicken Soup for the Soul*. He and his co-author committed to doing five things every day to promote the book—a process he terms the rule of five.[42] Sometimes they did small things, sometimes big. One time, they sent copies of their book to the jurors on the OJ Simpson trial, which was intended as a random act of kindness for the jurors who had been sequestered for a long time. One of the jurors was captured on film reading the book, and that inadvertently created great publicity.

> *I commit to doing five things every day*
> *to promote my new venture.*

TELL EVERYONE

This might seem obvious, but you need to tell everyone about your business—especially if you are launching a new product or service. In an age where we are bombarded with information, just because you've released a short statement on Facebook, doesn't mean that people have seen it. You need to repeat the news over and over and over again to capture people's attention. You don't have to act like you have a megaphone—just repeat the information and call to action consistently.

Jeanene Kennedy, the founder of wine and events business Winederlust, says that in her experience it's important to keep reiterating the message at every opportunity. 'It might feel spammy, but you can't assume that everyone has seen or heard your message,' she says. 'Algorithms on social media are changing all the time. It's likely only a small number of people see details so if you have something important like an event, you have to keep plugging it.'

A good place to start is by communicating with those you know. Tell the people who have supported you—your family, your friends and those who have helped in your business journey. Send them an email, ping them with a Facebook message, alert them on LinkedIn, call them on the phone or write them a letter—tell them, and even better, tell them personally, rather than through a bulk chain email. Let them know that you value their support and how passionate you are about what you are doing.

Also, share your business launch news on social media. Once again, it doesn't have to be perfect. Share small wins as they happen, such as the development of your logo, the manufacture of a prototype product, your first sale, and small yet significant milestones. I remember sharing a photo of Neil setting up the equipment ahead of recording *The Joyful Frugalista*. Then before too long, I was super proud to share there had been one hundred downloads, then one thousand. At the time of writing, there have been over sixty-three thousand downloads in less than two years, and most episodes now have over one thousand downloads. But that first milestone was significant, as it was a strong signal that what I was doing was working.

> *With joy in my heart, I tell everyone*
> *about my business offerings.*

LAUNCH PARTY

When *The Joyful Frugalista* was about to be published, many people asked me, 'When's the launch party?' And this is a common reaction you will receive when you tell people that you are about to launch a new business; everyone assumes there will be a party.

A launch party is often a good way for you to clarify what it is that you are now doing. You usually get to make a speech, sell a bit of product, and sometimes get media along. Even if you don't manage media, it's often great for social media.

The key disadvantage is that the people who come to your launch party won't necessarily be your long-term customers (although I would still recommend inviting them). Further, a launch party can be expensive. In the words of my husband, 'the people who come and drink your grog and eat your food might not buy your stuff.'

In our current pandemic world, there is also uncertainty around in-person events. It's important to have a COVID-safe plan, as well as a safety plan in general.

With *The Joyful Frugalista*, I was a bit unsure what to do about the launch. I naively assumed my publishers would organise one. They did a lot of things around the launch, but their focus was on media—not on an event. As I'd only organised and celebrated my wedding to Neil five months before the book came out, it felt weird to be inviting friends and family to another event where I would (again) be centrestage. But so many people said they wanted to come to a launch that eventually I decided to organise one.

We saw the book launch as a party and an opportunity to thank those who had been part of my journey. At one point, a friend suggested we hire a publicist to draw in local VIPs. But I decided to buck the trend and make it a fun and intimate event that was self-catered, aligned with my frugal values and a true celebration. What I wanted was to thank my community for supporting me on my writing journey.

Later, I found out that the more usual path is to hold an event at a local bookstore. Many of the bookstores in Canberra, where I live, are incredibly supportive of local authors. I participated in several events at bookstores, although none of them was a large launch as such. I also explored one bookstore for a catered launch, although it was a bit pricey—and crucially, they didn't have any dates or times that suited me or my audience. And I ruled out doing a launch at the National Library of Australia as I didn't think I'd have the huge pull needed to have a big event (nor was that my focus).

Having gone through this experience, I'm not totally against advising people to do a launch. But I do advise that, as with any event, you must be clear about your 'why'. Why are you holding the event? Is it to sell books or products? To get media attention? Or to celebrate with friends? Once you are clear on your purpose, you can then think about what venue, time and budget are appropriate. And above all, it's important to be clear about all the costs involved in the launch, as you are not likely to recoup them from sales.

I regret not being more strategic about the book launch. While there were speeches and photos, and I did sell almost enough books to cover the launch costs, I could have done a better job of building a community. I wish I had used the launch to add to my email list (perhaps via a lucky door prize), and above all, I wish I had asked my community to support me with reviews and testimonials. It is one thing for people to come to your launch party once; what you want is for them to be advocates for you and your business going forward.

FREEBIES

You've got your website, your product, your book or whatever it is you want to launch. How do you get people to know about it? One common way, especially with services, is to offer freebies.

Why give away things for free? Especially with things like coaching and advice, it's important to do trials so that you can refine what you are offering. It will build your confidence and hone your skills. You will find yourself talking about 'my clients' in no time.

But it's important to be strategic in how you give things away. Don't give things away to people who don't appreciate them. One way to make your giveaway impactful is to post in a group aligned with that subject or interest, and offer a session in exchange for a testimonial. The challenge here is to collect on the testimonial. I'm not sure why, but people are often extremely reluctant to write them. Or video them—video testimonials are fabulous and often even better than written ones.

You can ask people to share testimonials on your Google My Business account, Facebook or LinkedIn. If your product is a book, ask them to write a review on Goodreads or Amazon. Listeners of podcasts can leave reviews on Apple Podcasts. Why this is important is that it provides social proof of your business. Would you trust a business that you didn't know and seemed new? What about a business that had a testimonial from someone you knew?

INCENTIVES

A similar and related approach is offering a prize to people who promote your brand. For instance, you could ask people to share your book or services on Instagram or Facebook (tagging your social media handle) for a chance to win a prize.

I've successfully run campaigns where I have asked someone to tag a friend they would like to win the prize with (e.g. a dinner out for two, or a girls' shopping spree). This works especially well on Facebook pages, but note it doesn't work well in Facebook groups, as these are closed communities that do not allow you to tag people outside of the group.

More recently, I've seen podcasts promoted where people in the community are asked to join the 'launch party' or become a launch supporter. The idea is that you ask your community of supporters to share details about your launch, to follow/like and write reviews. You can reward them with points for each time they do this, with the points earned putting them in the running for a prize.

These incentives work well to a point, but it's important not to overuse them. At the end of the day, people will like your product or service because of its merits—not just because of an incentive program. But it is a great way of rallying your community by giving them a clear way to support you.

DISCOUNTS AND FLYERS

It's a good idea to offer discounts to celebrate a launch, as it encourages people to get onto your platform. For ecommerce options, it's generally easy to create a promo code (aka a coupon code) that you can share with your community. I find it best to send out promo codes in newsletters, or with your social media tribe. You want it to feel like it's a special offer, rather than have it on the main website (although in some cases you can do both). In other words, you want the promo code to be a drawcard for people coming to your website or business.

Depending on the business, you could also include details in a flyer that you drop off in your local neighbourhood. This works especially well for physical businesses. Your community will want to know about your fabulous new cafe with freshly roasted coffee, hair salon that can do school-formal hairstyles, or bakery with sourdough bread.

WORKING WITH INFLUENCERS

Through *The Joyful Frugalista*, I get approached to support emerging brands regularly. And back five or so years ago, I did a lot of food blogging and reviews and would get asked to support restaurant launches on a semi-regular basis.

Social media influencers can help make your business boom—but they can also cost you money and fail to make an impact.

There are, broadly, three types of influencers:

1. **Media personalities.** Think people who appear on television, are pop divas or frequently grace the cover of magazines. These people are recognisable household names, and their public endorsement of your product through things such as television advertisements can lend your product launch a significant boost. They rarely come cheap and are best used as part of a professional and coordinated marketing and PR campaign.

2. **Key opinion leaders (KOLs).** This refers to online influencers who have significant followers. By significant, I mean tens of thousands of followers—or even millions—on platforms such as YouTube, TikTok, Instagram and Facebook, and who have become professional or semi-professional. They will usually charge for their services and rarely do anything for free. A famous KOL in China is Austin Li Jiaqi (aka the Lipstick King). He recently sold USD1.7 billion in cosmetics within twelve hours as part of a special promotion.[43] You will generally have to pay or offer an affiliate relationship (or both) to secure the services of KOLs.

3. **Key opinion consumers (KOCs).** KOCS have fewer followers than KOLs. For many, their online presence is a hobby that they wish to grow. Some will charge for their services, while others

will promote items in exchange for freebies (or because your product or service aligns with their values, e.g. for sustainability/ environmental reasons). Increasingly, KOCs welcome the opportunity to be part of affiliate programs. You will not get the huge media or social-media splash you would get by working with the media or KOLs, but a key advantage is that KOCs usually have niche interests and loyal followers.

My foodie friends and I love going to restaurant launches. We love the special treatment, and I especially like meeting with the chef or owner and hearing about their vision. It seems easy: roll out the red carpet for social media influencers and then let them spread the word about how fabulous your business is—for free.

There are a few things to consider when working with influencers to ensure that it's a good experience for both of you:

1. **Build long-term rather than short-term relationships.** You might think, *Well, I'm giving them something for free, they should be grateful.* I'm always grateful for the generosity of business owners who invite me to restaurant or other launches. But the reality is that I spend hours editing photos, writing blog posts, and crafting and sharing social media posts. And I'm putting my reputation on the line. The value of the giveaway rarely compensates for the time and effort I put in. But I do it because I love it, and I especially love supporting local businesses or ventures. Often, I'll go back as a paying customer, or I will recommend it to others. More than the freebie, what I want is to connect with the 'why' of a business. A secondary goal is to use the experience to build my profile, so I want the business to share/give shoutouts about what I've written.

2. **Don't assume you can do anything with their content.** Unless you are paying for a professional photoshoot or copyediting, you do not own influencers' work. If you love an image and want to later use it as a major part of your branding, it would be appropriate to offer to pay for it (even if you've provided

the influencer a product or service for free). At the very least, it would be polite to ask first before using images or text in a major advertising campaign. And if you do end up using things without payment, such as re-sharing Instagram photos, make sure you attribute the source and send some love back through referrals.

3. **Don't dictate what the influencer can say, write or photograph.** Influencers retain their creative freedom and will produce what they feel is appropriate. Few will slam a business that has offered a freebie, but they probably won't say they like such and such a dish or product if they genuinely didn't like it. If you are brave enough, consider asking the influencer for constructive feedback on what could be improved. You might not like their answers, but better to hear from them now than get bad reviews.

4. **Provide details of your socials.** Make sure you provide influencers with details of your hashtags and social media handle/s, preferably in advance, so they can follow you and share. And make sure to like, share and comment on their social media posts as they come out.

5. **Be mindful of what you say to influencers.** Whatever you say to influencers is likely to find its way onto social media, so be careful not to relate anything confidential or inappropriate. I once went to a launch where the chef shared a funny story about a criminal syndicate and a historical link to his business premises. He had us in stitches of laughter. I made that the headline of my story and crafted the review around this history. The only problem was that he didn't want to talk about that publicly, so I had to do a major rewrite. (Note: In this case, I went back to the chef/owner with a draft—often, influencers won't.)

Working with social media influencers can help to build your online profile and get the word out, especially when you are new. It can also pave the way for more media, who are likely to google you before investigating further. You can also share social media reviews with newspapers or magazines when pitching that they review your business. But it's important to research your influencers carefully to make sure their message is a good fit, and organise the event professionally to avoid it turning into a free lunch with little impact.

MEDIA RELEASE

A media release (aka a press release) is a document that is sent to media or influencers and is easy for them to use in their stories. While simple to get right, it's easy to get wrong.

Journalists (and others in the industry, such as radio hosts) are busy people. They are often woefully underpaid and work to tight deadlines. They are under the pump to push out stories that people want to read, and rarely have time to sit and ponder.

A media release makes it easy for journalists to write a story that features you and your business. Journalists might just discover you randomly (it happens to me semi-regularly, especially if they've read a blog post or listened to a podcast). But usually, receiving a media release is the prompt for a story.

There are a few rules when it comes to drafting media releases:

1. **Keep it to one page.** Where possible, keep your media release short and sharp and limit it to one page. If a journalist wants to know more, they will contact you for an interview.

2. **Include your contact information.** This seems obvious, but I've written releases for other people where they are hesitant for their details to be made public. If you want a journalist to pick up your story, they need to be able to contact you.

3. **Be responsive.** You also need to keep your channels of communication open for around twenty-four hours after you send out a media release. Take your phone off silent, check your email regularly and respond promptly.

4. **Use direct quotes.** A good media release contains quotes

attributable to someone important (e.g. the founder or CEO). For instance: 'I'm proud to serve as Australia's Ambassador for Women's Entrepreneurship Day, and I'm passionate about helping female entrepreneurs shine,' said Serina. You want to make it easy for a journalist to lift out those quotes and put them into an article, with the result sounding like they conducted a one-on-one interview.

5. **Include photos.** Always include high-quality photos where possible. Generally, landscape photos are preferred for online news articles and portraits for Instagram. Don't attach too many to an email, as it makes it large and unwieldy to send and view. Do send via the cloud, but make sure the photos are easy to retrieve. *HerCanberra* editor Beatrice Smith says she prefers Dropbox as it's generally easier to open and use. 'So often people send me images via Google Drive but have forgotten to make the link accessible,' she says. 'Having to go back and forth to get a shareable link so that I can download the image means time and effort.'

6. **Have a newsworthy subject.** Journalists can receive hundreds of media releases a week. A media release about how XYZ is a nice business is unlikely to make it over the line. The topic or theme needs to be something that a media outlet's audience wants to hear about. Do they want to know about local businesses that have won a big award? Scored a big contract? Released a new report? Or are maybe planning a big event? Make the media release subject newsworthy.

7. **Avoid sounding like an infomercial.** There's a difference between a genuine news article and a piece of puffery. If your story sounds like an ad, you will probably need to purchase one. Most news outlets will have options for paid (versus earnt) media, and some are surprisingly well-written sponsored posts. Be respectful of their business and don't feed them spam.

8. **Personalise the email attaching the media release.** Don't just

send your email out to everyone on your list in a spray-and-pray approach. Instead, take some time to understand the likely focus of the journalist you are talking to and explain why your story is relevant to their audience. For example, when sharing information about the Zonta Club of Canberra Breakfast's Pre-loved Fashion Sale, I emphasise the support for domestic violence victims, fashion, or sustainability, depending on who I send the release to.

HIRING A PR COMPANY OR PUBLICIST

Many people fundamentally don't understand what public relations, aka PR, is about. According to Candice Meisels from Candice PR, PR is about how you manage the dissemination of information between your business and internal and external stakeholders. Internal stakeholders are your employees; this is your internal communication and brand values. Meanwhile, external stakeholders are your customers, the media, shareholders and investors.

Candice says that PR can be powerful because it can build:

1. Brand awareness
2. Credibility
3. Search Engine Optimization (SEO)
4. Social media followers
5. You or your spokesperson's profile as an industry expert

A PR professional or publicist has many tools at their disposal, a chief one being knowing who to send a media release to. PR companies invest in developing contacts, and a good PR company is well connected. A PR company can also help you shape your message and get your word out. They are usually good copywriters and know how to write a media release that gets attention.

My publisher hired an external publicist for the launch of *The Joyful Frugalista*. She scored me a spot on *Sunrise*, radio interviews with ABC—

including an interview with Patricia Karvelas on Radio National Drive (plus regional ABC stations around the country)—and ensured extracts were in *Reader's Digest* and the *Daily Mail*. And those are just the ones I remember—the launch was a busy time. My publicist's contacts and connections were pivotal in ensuring I received media coverage in addition to what I was already attracting.

PAID ADVERTISEMENTS

There are now many options for paid advertisements beyond print media, radio, and television. That said, depending on your audience, these might still be relevant. Television, for instance, became surprisingly affordable for a while during COVID. And radio can be extremely effective in reaching people, especially as many people listen to the radio while commuting or at work. People listen to the radio intently during national crises such as bushfires, as it's often the only available mode of communication.

Social media has opened up new advertisement pathways. A relatively easy one is Facebook Ads, which allows you to boost content or a Facebook page. I often find it more effective to boost the page itself rather than a post, as you want to convert people into longer-term followers than have them just read one article. That said, if a post is trending better on average than others, Facebook will nudge you and suggest you spend money to boost it. An advantage of Facebook Ads is that they are relatively low in cost and allow you to tailor your ad to key demographics (e.g. local area, gender, age, and themes).

With most people using Google to search the internet, investing in Google Ads can be effective—especially for digital businesses. You want your business to appear prominently in Google searches, so why not work with Google? But it's important not to just throw money at Google Ads—you need to know what you are doing, and have a clear idea of your budget and desired outcome. Above all, you want to have a product or service that people are likely to want to search for on Google.

DON'T STOP BELIEVING

Not all launches go to plan, and not all businesses blossom as you expect. If your launch isn't getting the huge traction you were expecting, the important thing is to keep believing in yourself and your ability to be in business. Successful business owners have been through many ups and downs. They know that if something doesn't work, it's important to reflect on what the problems are and then tweak and refine your approach. You might find, for instance, that you aren't showing up enough for your community on social media. Or that your tribe is not where you thought it would be.

EXERCISES

1.

What product or service could you pre-sell?
Write down a list of things that you could begin
selling now.

2.

What is holding you back from starting to pre-sell
your product or service? Write down some of the
emotional and practical obstacles you have to pre-
selling. Look at what you have written down. Are
these real issues, or are they excuses?

3.

Commit to doing one thing to start pre-selling
(e.g. talk about it at a networking group, do a
Facebook Live about it, sign up for Kickstarter or
post on social media).

4.

Write down five things you could do to launch your
product. Dare yourself to think creatively.

5.

Draft a media release—even if your product or
service isn't ready yet.

6.

Share updates about your progress on your social
media channels.

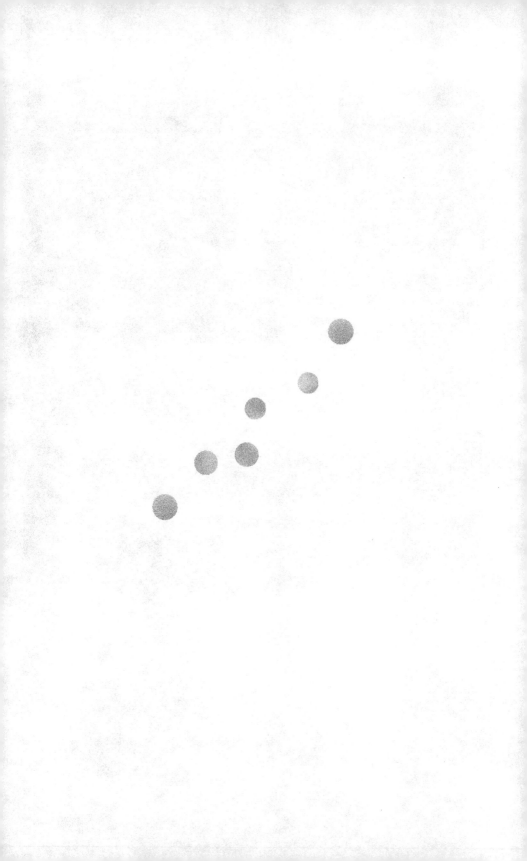

Acknowledgements

I would like to thank my husband, Neil Hadley, for being there to support me pursuing my entrepreneurial dreams, for listening to me vent (about myriad things!) and for reading every word of this book and finding errors I had missed.

Thank you to the Canberra Innovation Network for creating an empowering and enabling community that has given me the confidence to go forth and write this book. Many of the Facebook Lives on which this book is based were recorded there, and I met many of the people I have quoted in this book through the Network and related community events.

To all of the many gurus who contributed their knowledge in this book, quoted or unquoted—thank you. This includes: April Mack, Amy Bett, Angie Rassie, Anton Pemmer, Aranka Nolan, Avril Henry, Bea Smith, Bec Cuzzillo, Bec McFarland, Bushy Martin, Cindy Mitchell, Claire Harris, Craig Davis, Damien Hollingsworth, Geoff Mether, Jacqui Owen, Janine Linklater, Jeanene Kennedy, Kellie Nissen, Kurt Walkom, Lib Ferreira, Litsa Barberoglou, Liz Fry Walton, Marg Lange, Marg Wade, Michelle, Misty Henkel, Mitch Barbara, Nick McNaughton, Nick Nicolaides, Noel Whittaker, Paul Boultwood, Rachel Service, Rae Knopik, Rebecca Tregurtha, Ronni Kahn, Sheree Henley, Steve Gregory, Susie Basiaco, Suzy Cherub, Theme Rains, Theresa Gattung and Wendy Marman.

Special thanks to Natasha Gilmour at the kind press and her publishing team for believing in me and this project. And to the amazing Georgia Jordan for her thorough editing.

I also wish to thank Jelena Josipovic for proofreading several chapters and providing advice.

I was writing this during a time of negative energy as a result of COVID and a project going off course due to a shonky website developer. I could have easily given up. Special thanks to reiki energy healer and intuit Katya Dantini, and to my business coach Bec McFarland of Pop! Your Business.

And finally, special thanks to you—my reader—for buying or borrowing this book. I wish you every possible success with your startup or business. We are living in times of unprecedented disruption and global threats. But also in a time of unprecedented opportunity. More than ever, we need people with a vision for heart-centred enterprises to help heal the world. This book is intended as a gift to help guide you to where you need to be while avoiding some of the common pitfalls (including ones I have faced).

About the Author

SERINA BIRD

Serina Bird is passionate about helping women save money, live their dreams, and shine at their full potential. In 2019, Serina left her diplomatic career in search of living aligned with purpose. She is now founder of *The Joyful Frugalista, The Joyful Fashionista* and *The Joyful Business Club* and serves as Women's Entrepreneurship Day Organisation Australia Country Ambassador. She hosts regular interviews on business topics in The Joyful Business Club, and is currently leaning into a new-found love of tech and ecommerce. Serina has also been featured on ABC Radio National and *Sunrise,* and in the *Sun-Herald, Money magazine* and News.com.au.

Serina is author of *The Joyful Frugalista: Grow Your Cash, Be Savvy with Your Money and Live Abundantly.* Serina's second book, *The Joyful Startup Guide,* shares tried-and-true tips for cultivating a business that is successful, sustainable, and highly rewarding.

Connect with *The Joyful Business Club* on Facebook and LinkedIn.

Notes

1 *Think and Grow Rich* by Napoleon Hill, p. 127

2 'Why Every Entrepreneur Should Take an 8-Hour Shower Each Week: The benefits of creative time', entrepreneur.com/article/365362

3 'Why We Have Our Best Ideas in the Shower: The science of creativity', buffer.com/resources/shower-thoughts-science-of-creativity

4 asic.gov.au/for-business/registering-a-business-name

5 business.gov.au/planning/business-structures-and-types/business-structures/partnership

6 business.gov.au/registrations/register-licences-and-permits

7 *Think and Grow Rich* by Napoleon Hill, p. 129

8 *Think and Grow Rich* by Napoleon Hill, p. 149

9 'How supercool Australian social enterprise brand Thankyou is inviting P&G and Unilever (and many others) to collaborate to end extreme poverty', forbes.com/sites/afdhelaziz/2020/10/29/how-supercool-australian-social-enterprise-brand-thank-you-is-inviting-pg-and-unilever-and-many-others-to-collaborate-to-end-extreme-poverty

10 'Fund-raiser Thankyou Water drops support for evangelical group', smh.com.au/national/fund-raiser-thankyou-water-drops-support-for-evangelical-group-20130820-2s987.html

11 'How supercool Australian social enterprise brand Thankyou is inviting P&G and Unilever (and many others) to collaborate to end extreme poverty', forbes.com/sites/afdhelaziz/2020/10/29/how-supercool-australian-social-enterprise-brand-thank-you-is-inviting-pg-and-unilever-and-many-others-to-collaborate-to-end-extreme-poverty
12 '2021 Trusted Brands Australia winners', trustedbrands.com.au/results.asp

13 'Weet-Bix relaunches in China as customers pay up to $50 a box', theaustralian.com.au/business/companies/weetbix-pushes-further-into-china-as-customers-pay-up-to-50-a-box/news-story/a91af6139e8ef053eb362d65bad40161

14 'Zappos Culture: A corporate culture success story', hiring.monster.com/resources/workforce-management/company-culture/corporate-culture-zappos

15 'Zappos' sneaky strategy for hiring the best people involves a van ride from the airport to the interview', businessinsider.com.au/zappos-sneaky-strategy-for-hiring-the-best-people-2015-12

16 'AstraZeneca's COVID-19 vaccine rebranding to "Vaxzevria" ahead of international travel restart', abc.net.au/news/2021-08-06/astrazeneca-vaccine-rebrand-vaxzevria-covid-9/100356980

17 'The $35 Nike logo and the woman who designed it', creativemarket.com/blog/the-35-nike-logo-and-the-woman-who-designed-it

18 'Learn to love networking', hbr.org/2016/05/learn-to-love-networking
19 'Elizabeth Holmes: Theranos founder convicted of fraud', bbc.com/news/world-us-canada-59734254

20 'Win people over with 2 simple, powerful FBI tactics', inc.com/carmine-gallo/win-people-over-with-2-simple-powerful-fbi-tactics.html

21 ato.gov.au/Individuals/Income-and-deductions/Deductions-you-can-claim/Self-education-expenses

22 'A list of Australian venture capital firms', fundcomb.com/blog/a-list-of-australian-vcs

23 'Pinky Gloves are just the latest ludicrous attempt to monetise the vagina', theguardian.com/commentisfree/2021/apr/21/pinky-gloves-are-just-the-latest-ludicrous-attempt-to-monetise-the-vagina

24 Ibid.

25 'The tampon removal glove created by men that got investor backing is an example of a broken system', womensagenda.com.au/latest/the-tampon-removal-glove-created-by-men-that-got-investor-backing-is-an-example-of-a-broken-system/

26 'Crowdfunding for mum entrepreneurs', readyfundgo.com/crowdfunding-is-a-great-way-to-test-your-business-idea-and-get-started-today

27 asic.gov.au/regulatory-resources/financial-services/crowd-sourced-funding

28 'What is a partnership?', lawpath.com.au/blog/what-is-a-partnership

29 slicingpie.com

30 'How to find the perfect co-founder, according to five Startmate Alumni who've been there, done that', startmate.com/writing/how-to-find-co-founder

31 'How former beauty editor Zoë Foster Blake built a $177m empire', afr.com/young-rich/how-former-beauty-editor-zoe-foster-blake-built-a-177m-empire-20210827-p58mho

32 'How to find the perfect co-founder, according to five Startmate Alumni who've been there, done that', startmate.com/writing/how-to-find-co-founder

33 *The Tao of Pooh* by Benjamin Hoff, 1982

34 'How multitasking affects productivity and brain health', verywellmind.com/multitasking-2795003

35 Ibid.

36 'The secrets to staying productive when you have a big project', themuse.com/advice/the-secrets-to-staying-productive-when-you-have-a-big-project

37 'The Rule of 52 and 17: It's random, but it ups your productivity', themuse.com/advice/the-rule-of-52-and-17-its-random-but-it-ups-your-productivity

38 'The agreement that catapulted Microsoft over IBM', ozy.com/true-and-stories/the-agreement-that-catapulted-microsoft-over-ibm

39 'The Rise of DOS: How Microsoft got the IBM PC OS contract', au.pcmag.com/operating-systems/88773/the-rise-of-dos-how-microsoft-got-the-ibm-pc-os-contract

40 'The agreement that catapulted Microsoft over IBM', ozy.com/true-and-stories/the-agreement-that-catapulted-microsoft-over-ibm

41 'The agreement that catapulted Microsoft over IBM', ozy.com/true-and-stories/the-agreement-that-catapulted-microsoft-over-ibm

42 'Jack Canfield shares the rule of five', youtu.be/pG7q05cjpY4

43 'China's Lipstick King sold an astonishing $1.7 billion in goods in 12 hours—and that was just in a promotion for the country's biggest shopping day', businessinsider.com.au/china-lipstick-king-sold-17-billion-stuff-in-12-hours-2021-10

CPSIA information can be obtained
at www.ICGtesting.com
Printed in the USA
LVHW021026170322
713598LV00007B/530